HOWARD
BOOKS

The
TEN-SECOND
PRAYER
PRINCIPLE

PRAYING POWERFULLY AS YOU GO

Mark Littleton

HOWARD BOOKS
A DIVISION OF SIMON & SCHUSTER
New York London Toronto Sydney

Our purpose at Howard Books is to:

- *Increase faith* in the hearts of growing Christians
- *Inspire holiness* in the lives of believers
- *Instill hope* in the hearts of struggling people everywhere

Because He's coming again!

Published by Howard Books, a division of Simon & Schuster, Inc.
1230 Avenue of the Americas, New York, NY 10020
www.howardpublishing.com

The Ten-Second Prayer Principle © 2007 by Mark Littleton

Library of Congress Cataloging-in-Publication Data

Littleton, Mark.
   The ten-second prayer principle : praying powerfully as you go / Mark Littleton.
     p. cm.
   Summary: "A simple how-to book with sixteen practical principles offers ways of improving one's prayer time"—Provided by publisher.
   1. Prayer—Christianity. I. Title.
   BV215.L58 2007
   248.3'2—dc22

2007017420

ISBN-13: 978-1-4165-4191-2
ISBN-10:   1-4165-4191-8

10 9 8 7 6 5 4 3 2 1

For information regarding special discounts for bulk purchases, please contact: Simon & Schuster Special Sales at 1-800-456-6798 or business@simonandschuster.com.

Edited by Between the Lines
Cover design by David Uttley
Interior design by Jaime Putorti

To Jeanette, who teaches me about prayer every day.

To Nicole, for whom I pray every day.

To Alisha, who seems to be learning about the power of prayer every day.

To Gardner, who lets me pray with him every night, even though he'd probably rather play his Nintendo DS.

To Elizabeth, who, at only three years old, listens to me pray for her every night and then gives me a nice, wet kiss.

CONTENTS

CONTENTS

CONFESSIONS OF A LOUSY PRAY-ER

Probably the shortest prayer most Christians pray regularly is "Lord, help!"

I've prayed that prayer many times. Like when I can't find my keys—which happens about once a week. Or when I can't find other things—my three-year-old, for instance, when I'm in the mall. How is it that she manages to sneak off so easily? Oh, it's because I'm not watching her *every single second*. Yes, we fathers do need some remedial instruction when it comes to parenting three-year-olds.

I know the power of a short, solid, concise, and heartfelt prayer.

"Uh, Lord, do you have any recommendations about this ant problem in my house?"

"Seriously, God, would you do something about this traffic situation? I want to get home."

"By the way, Jesus . . . could you direct me to a parking space? I'd rather not have to walk four miles in this heat to take my daughter to buy a sports bra."

And, "Really, Lord, won't you do something about the Kansas City Royals? They're losing like crazy out there. They stink to high heaven. I'll bet you can even smell them."

Short, quick prayers without big spiritual ramifications are my specialty. But what about longer, pastoral, in-depth, heartfelt, and passionate prayers of greater consequence? Prayers that go on for hours pleading and interceding to really get action from God? (Unlike His answers about the Royals.)

That kind of prayer is really tough. And here's where my confession comes in: I've never been able to pray for large blocks of time. When I say "large blocks," I'm talking about fifteen minutes or more—straight, unwavering, God-centered prayer, every day over a long period of time, say, several months. Usually, when I get down on my knees to pray (or sit in my easy chair or lie on my bed), I run out of ideas in five to ten minutes. I can praise, petition, confess, give thanks, and all that, but when I glance at my watch, fewer than five minutes have crawled by.

The one method I've used to help me pray longer is to pray when I walk for exercise. But since I don't walk every day, and since illnesses and other problems can halt my exercise program, interruptions wreak havoc on my prayer life. If I can't keep my eyes open and my feet in motion, I lose my focus and concentration in prayer.

Years ago I read a statement, I'm not sure by whom, that has always stuck with me: "I have so much to do today that I'll have to spend the first three hours in prayer or the devil will get the victory."

Three hours? Of prayer? In the morning, when my brain is foggy as Seattle in April?

I decided long ago that if that was what it took to keep the devil from getting the victory in my life, then he was practically guaranteed a heyday with me.

I also read great books about David Brainerd, John Wesley, John "Praying" Hyde, and others who prayed for hours at a time. One entry in Brainerd's famous diary told of his lying in the snow and praying with such passion that he melted the snow around him and afterward rose up in a sweat.

Rather than inspiring me to pray more, these stories only amplified my miserable feelings of failure. I could never hope to measure up to such powerful examples of intercession.

Some years ago I read that the average pastor spends about seven minutes a day in prayer. I was horrified—for about a second. And then it struck me: how was I any better than them?

Over the years, as the guilt piled up, I wondered what was wrong with me.

I come to those scriptures that talk about Jesus's getting up early in the morning to pray, and I feel delinquent. I stumble on the texts that say he prayed all night before embarking on some new direction in his ministry. When I compare myself with him, I'm conscience-stricken at my lack of spirituality.

Have you ever felt that way?

If so, then this book is for you. I'll show you how to build a tremendous prayer life in small bits—both easy to bite off and easy to swallow. You'll see that such prayers can be incredibly powerful and spiritually fulfilling.

Let me tell you about something that happened recently. My seven-year-old got into kids' collector cards and games last year. I didn't think much about it, and I heard nothing negative from other parents; nor did I see anything negative about it in my reading. But my son was terrorized every night by bad dreams. He imagined monsters in the dark. I began praying short, clipped prayers of desperation and befuddlement: "Lord, please help Gardner get over this, and please help me and Jeanette [my wife] to know how to deal with this." I had no idea what the underlying problem was. This went on for about a month.

Then one night Gardner staggered into our bedroom crying and terribly frightened. Shivering, he crawled into bed between me and Jeanette and lay there sobbing his little heart out. After some comforting and gentle questioning, he told us, "Satan keeps tricking me. I see demons in the dark. I'm really scared, Dad. He's going to get me."

We questioned him more, trying to get to the bottom of things. Had he seen something harmful on television? Had he seen a scary movie? What books had he been reading? We had to figure out why these terrors had come upon him and take steps to ease them. "It's those cards and games," he suddenly confessed after a barrage of our fruitless queries. "They have spells. And the spells make you see monsters."

Believe me, that word *spells* horrified me. I thought the cards, games, and videos we bought for our children were harmless, but suddenly it seemed our son was involved in occult activities.

We talked to him gently, and suddenly he said, "I want to accept Jesus." He had never said that before, though we'd talked to him about faith in Christ. I led him in a prayer, and when we were done, he said, "I don't feel afraid now."

Over the next week, Gardner spoke of Jesus in his life.

I was astonished . . . and grateful . . . and overjoyed. We took away all the games and cards related to this set. He hasn't seen any more monsters in the dark, and he's been much happier since then.

As I reflect on our prayers in the midst of that situation, I realize now that they didn't include lying on the floor begging. No fasting, no long hours of pleading and making our case: nothing but a sweet, short, simple prayer in the dark. It took us less than a minute to utter.

I had thought Gardner was having a normal, seven-year-old problem. But God knew the real nature of the problem, and though my prayer was small, what a whopper of an answer! And God responded quickly. It's not often that I see prayers answered with barely a pause at the end before God's resounding reply.

Yet I do think it's the heartfelt utterances in the middle of the night, the sobbed one-sentence prayers at a sickbed, and the keening cries for help out of the pit of despair that often get God's swiftest responses. Perhaps our cries of desperation are more eloquent to God than any long-winded pulpit prayers that cover everything but matter little.

I believe that for most people, short, earnest prayers sent heavenward while driving or exercising are just as important—and a lot more manageable—than spending hours in prayer each morning.

Please understand: I don't mean to knock people who pray for long stretches of time. I revere those people. But for most of us, such lengthy praying is next to impossible. Not only do we not have sufficient stretches of time to do it, but even if we did, we'd quickly run out of things to say.

My goal is to show you how being a ten-second prayer warrior has enabled me to pray about all kinds of specific, consequential issues without having to stop the car and kneel under the dashboard or even bow my head. I can "shoot off" a prayer to God in my mind in just seconds. I've found that not only does he hear such prayers, but he often answers them quickly and positively.

I also hope to show that you can learn to pray for longer periods, and even pray in groups, without getting bored. But that's putting the goal before the game.

If you dread the prayer part of your quiet time, I'd like to share with you some wonderful principles of prayer that are simple and effective yet biblical and spiritually powerful.

CHAPTER ONE

THE TEN-SECOND PRAYER PRINCIPLE

Tom never thought of himself as a prayer warrior. In fact, he never thought about himself as being much of anything except a regular guy who loved his family, his church, and his country.

He had a decent job: he was a middle manager at a local telecommunications company. He had a nice family: loving wife and three relatively well-adjusted and happy kids. He had fun with his family on vacation a couple of times each year. He was actively involved at church too. He taught a Sunday-school class, usually working through a book of the Bible in five, ten, or more weeks. He studied his Bible, although sometimes he knew he relied too much on the curriculum notes the church gave him.

He was faithful in all those areas.

But Tom had picked up a unique concept about prayer early in his Christian life. He liked it because it gave him a way to pray without getting bogged down in minutiae or struggling to keep his mind from wandering when he tried to pray for longer periods. He had heard it called "praying without ceasing" and "the ten-second prayer," but the fact that it was short and quick made it easy for him to utter many prayers in the course of a day.

The thought of praying for ten seconds was appealing to him. It was manageable. It broke things down into bite-size chunks that kept him active in the prayer arena. Ten-second prayers were the only way he could do it. After all, his knees had given out when he played high-school football, and kneeling caused him tremendous pain. He didn't think God was too stuck on that particular posture for praying, since the Bible so rarely specified that anyone prayed on his knees.

Getting up earlier in the morning was out of the question for Tom too. If he didn't get his eight hours of sleep, he felt worthless all day. He rarely managed to turn in before eleven at night, so to awaken earlier than seven would be tough. He knew having a quiet time was important, but he'd found ways to get it done other than rising early. He simply chose not to let others' championing the early morning hours bother him. He knew God had made everyone unique, and if he had a different way of doing things, if it kept him growing in his love for God, what did it matter if he didn't do it the way some people said it should be done?

Let me take you through part of Tom's day to show you how the ten-second prayer principle works.

When the alarm clock shocked him from sleep at 7 a.m., Tom eased his aching limbs over the edge of the bed and sat for a moment, rubbing his temples. "Thanks for a good night's sleep, Lord," he murmured, and then staggered toward the bathroom.

Ten-second prayer number one.

As he stood before the bathroom mirror, he turned on the water and splashed some on his face. It was still cold, so he shivered and said, "Ah, that feels good, Lord. Thanks for cold water and the refreshment it gives me."

Ten-second prayer number two.

He reached into the shower and turned on the water, catching a glimpse of himself in the mirror. He knew he was no prize, but he smiled, pulled in his tummy, and said, "One of these days I'm going to get a perfect body, right, Lord? So I've got something to look forward to, don't I. Help me keep up with the exercises, OK? Sometimes it isn't easy to get it done."

Ten-second prayer number three.

He stepped into the shower and let the water cascade over him comfortingly, its warmth radiating deep into his muscles, soothing his aches, washing away the morning's fog. "That feels great, Lord. Thanks for the hot water and that the water heater is holding up. Please help it to hold out through the year: I just don't have the money to replace it or make a major repair . . . unless you want to send me a windfall."

Ten- second prayer number four.

As Tom showered, he prayed for other situations that came to his mind, racking up prayers five, six, and seven.

Tom opened the bathroom door to let the moisture escape and came face to face with his wife, Darla, head-ing to the kitchen for the day's first cup of coffee. He smiled affectionately at her and prayed silently, "Thank you, Lord, for that woman, who looks beautiful even first thing in the morning. Please give us many years together."

Ten-second prayer number eight.

"What're you so happy about?" Darla asked.

"I was just telling God how thankful I am to have such a beautiful wife."

"Amen," she said before moving on with a step Tom thought was a little bit lighter.

Tom turned back to the sink to brush his teeth. As he squeezed the speckled paste onto his toothbrush, he remembered his father-in-law's complaint about how much his false teeth were hurting him. As he brushed, Tom prayed in his mind, "Help Dad not to have such problems with his teeth, Lord. Whatever it takes. And if he needs to buy new dentures, help him find the money he'll need. If I can help out, let me know."

Ten-second prayer number nine.

Finally his mind turned to his job. What a wreck that was. He didn't like where he worked, who he worked for, or how things had turned out. Great promises had been made at the start, but none had been kept. He stared at his tired-looking eyes in the mirror, then murmured, "God, please guide me. I don't know what to do about my job. I'm unhappy, and I need a change, but I'm scared. Lead me. I've got bills to pay."

That was all he said. He told himself that God knew what was in his heart, so no long explanation was necessary. But then something else occurred to him and he added, "But Lord, as long as I'm there, help me to do a good job. That's all I ask."

~

Don't you get the feeling that Tom enjoyed his prayer life? No dullness, no repeating the same old stuff: He constantly tilled new ground. Everything that came his way turned into an opportunity for prayer. That's the essence of prayer that never ends. In 1 Thessalonians 5:17 Paul seemed to be advocating such a prayer life when he said, "Pray without ceasing."

Someone recently told me that the "without ceasing"

part of that verse was used in other contexts to refer to a medical condition that kept coming back. Perhaps even Paul himself had such a condition, though we don't know for sure. The application, though, is clear: Keep coming back to those previous prayers. Don't give up on them. Repeat, revise, reform. But never give up until it's clear that God says, "No," or you realize the Spirit leading you in another direction.

Another person told me that "without ceasing" was a concept similar to a hacking cough. Ever had one of them? You cough. Stop. Then cough again. And again. And again.

Now, I don't want to give you a hacking cough. I just want to convey the idea of something that's ongoing— that persists no matter what we happen to be doing. Prayer without ceasing simply means we never sign off with God. We come back to the thoughts, needs, concerns, and situations in our lives, at home, and in our world time after time. Every few minutes or so, we might think of something that needs to be prayed about. So we send a brief "heavenly telegram" to God.

Tom had a flourishing prayer life and a close relationship with God despite the fact that he didn't start the day with thirty or forty minutes in his "prayer closet." He talked to God naturally, without premeditation or planning, taking cues from life—from whatever was happening around him at any given moment—as prompts for prayer.

Most of his prayers were less than ten seconds each. Yet the nine prayers he uttered just in the process of getting up and showering added up to . . . well, who cares how much time? What's the point in crunching numbers? It was fun. Fulfilling. Relational. Real. Easy. And it wasn't time consuming. These prayers came up in the course of the morning as naturally as thinking about his day, setting some goals, and planning his activities.

Most of all, Tom's prayers covered a lot of ground. Not the same old stuff. Not the typical prayers we all tend to repeat. He prayed about many different things, and in many different postures—on the bed, in the shower, at the sink, pulling on his shirt. He was praying without ceasing.

How can you do this throughout your day? How can you begin to create a lifestyle of prayer that permeates everything you do?

Such a lifestyle springs from a mentality that says, "Prayer is important. Praying for others—even people and things I don't know personally—changes the world. Therefore, I will pray as much as I can every day."

Praying without ceasing occurs in the context of the natural unfolding of our day. We don't have to go to a special place, kneel, and rigidly follow some prayer formula or cutesy acrostic. No, we can pray naturally and effortlessly: like breathing. The moment we become aware of something—a blessing, a need, an opportunity—we immediately mention it to God: in our minds, out loud, or in any way we want. And God will hear us. His promise is, "All things for which you pray and ask, believe that you have received them, and they will be granted you" (Mark 11:24).

God clearly beckons us to pray as often as we think to do so. He promises to answer, even those ten-second prayers we soon after forget. God doesn't forget.

Years ago I taught a large Sunday school class in a local church. One Sunday a couple, Tony and Carole, arrived bubbling over with questions about my lesson, about the reality of God, and about how God works in our lives. I answered, and as I did, I prayed, "Lord, these people are real. Help me minister to them."

That was it. Another Sunday Tony and Carole invited me to lunch, where we engaged in deeper and more difficult questions, but I didn't think about my prayer again until much later. That's when Carole told me, "I love the way you teach. You're the most realistic, honest Christian I've ever met."

It was the start of a friendship with both of them that has lasted many years. I think it all began because of one moment of prayer I'd quickly forgotten. Fortunately, God hadn't. In fact, over the next two years, God led me into a deeper and more extensive friendship with this couple, and they helped me through a harrowing episode of my life with understanding that came directly from their own similar experience.

Here's another example of the Ten-Second Prayer Principle at work. We have a hamster. My wife and I can't seem to get it through our three-year-old daughter Elizabeth's head that letting Fluffy out of her cage is dangerous. Why? Because we have two cats and two dogs, each of them hungry for hamster flesh.

One day Fluffy got out because nobody noticed when Elizabeth left the door open. Fluffy disappeared without a trace. The moment we discovered her absence, I prayed, "Lord, bring Fluffy out into the open so we can catch her, please—and before the cats or dogs get her."

Every day when I got up in the morning, before we left the house, when we returned, and when I turned out the lights before bed, I looked for Fluffy. She had to be getting hungry, so I repeated, "Lord, whenever you're ready, just fling her out here."

Then one night we walked into the house, and there was Fluffy, in the middle of the family room. Covered with saliva. The dog hovered over her and clearly had gotten her into her mouth but decided she wasn't quite as tasty as she looked.

I grabbed her and put her back into her cage. That was it. But I also sent a mental note to God: "Thanks, Lord. You did good."

That's just one of many types of prayers I see answered all the time in our household. Wouldn't it be exciting to see real, regular, and powerful answers to your prayers? Nearly every day? On all kinds of levels?

And won't it be amazing to get to heaven and find out that all those things you prayed about in passing came to pass? God will have answered every one, even those you forgot.

If that possibility excites you, read on. I want to show you much more.

CHAPTER TWO

THE CREATIVITY PRINCIPLE

Tom strode downstairs to breakfast feeling invigorated and ready for the problems he knew he'd face at work. His job had reached a crossroads. As he entered the kitchen, he prayed again about that situation, then sat at the table. He poured himself a bowl of Cheerios and whispered, "Great stuff, Lord. Thanks. I even hear they're good for lowering cholesterol."

"What'd you say, honey?" Darla asked as she stood in the kitchen doorway and called to their three children to hurry.

"Just thanking God for a great breakfast." And in his mind, he added, "Give Darla a pleasant breakfast too, and put the kids in a cheerful mood. That would be nice."

The kids filed into the kitchen. Ginny was eleven, with brown hair and bright blue eyes. She had her heart set on a spot on the sixth-grade basketball team. Brad, nine, had blond hair, like his mom, and an acute case of soccer-craziness. Abigail was five and a little charmer. As the children talked to Darla, Tom prayed for them in his mind again, asking God to shower his grace on them, to be with them at school, and to give each one a good day.

"Father, help Brad to play soccer well and to really get this math stuff down in school."

"Jesus, give Ginny some real encouragement. Even if she doesn't win the top position on the basketball team, let her find satisfaction and joy in whatever she does play."

"God, show Abby how much we all love her."

As he ate, Tom scanned the kitchen, thinking about how Darla longed for the money to do a major overhaul, with new cabinets and appliances. "Lord," he mouthed silently, "make that happen someday soon."

Ginny must have seen Tom's lips move and said, "Dad, you praying again?"

"Sort of."

The mail lay on the table for him to riffle through. He picked up a letter from an investment firm that handled several accounts he and Darla were building up to pay for the kids' college education. As he opened it, he prayed, "Father, help us to continue adding to these accounts, and let the investments do well in the markets. I'm not asking for a windfall—though that would be nice—but whatever you can do would be great."

Finishing his cereal, Tom dropped the paper and tilted a book Ginny appeared to be reading so he could see the cover. "Good book?" he asked.

"No, it's just something for school."

"Are you learning anything?"

"It's about Columbus, Dad."

"Well, he was important."

"Not to me."

Tom laughed and headed for the front door. On the way he prayed, "Father, give my daughter a love for knowledge and reading. And help us all to keep a good sense of humor."

Darla stood near the door with paper towels and a

spray bottle in her hands. "Good-bye, babe," she said, kissing his cheek.

"Something happen?" he asked, nodding to the cleaning supplies.

"I have to clean up a mess the dog made in the family room."

"Ew, sorry."

"She's getting old, that's all."

They'd raised Angelina from a pup, but that was many years ago. It would be hard to say good-bye to the loving, gentle dog, but Tom knew that day would come. As he thought about it, another prayer popped into his mind: "Lord, please give Jody a gentle end of life, and help the kids through it. Losing her will hit them hardest."

Then, on reflection, he added, "But not until it's time. Give us as much time with her as possible."

When he reached the car, Tom winged one more prayer aloft. "Keep everyone safe today, Lord. Let us feel your presence. And help me at work today. It'll be tedious, but help me to do my best."

As you can see, Tom's a fairly creative guy when it comes to prayer, but his methodology reveals a powerful principle: As we learn to pray about the things we encounter throughout our day, we'll become more creative and personal too.

Have you ever wondered what God thinks of us when we offer up to him the same stale, tried-and-dull words that come more easily than when we truly think about what we're saying?

One night when she was about thirteen, my daughter Alisha said to me as I began to pray for her (I do this every night with my kids), "Dad, you always pray the same thing for me."

I shook my head. "I always pray that you'll have a good night's sleep and a good day tomorrow, but I also pray about something specific that I know happened today that you mentioned and I noticed. If you listen, you'll see that I do that in every prayer."

"Okay," she said, and as I prayed, I mentioned the very things we'd just discussed. I waited for her response when I finished, and she said, "Yeah, I guess you did do what you say. I'll have to listen more closely from now on."

"What I want to know is if God's answering."

"Well," she said thoughtfully, "I usually get a good night's sleep. And most of the time school is pretty fun. And I'm learning things. The other thing about my friend Meghan, I'll watch for an answer to that one."

Over the years Alisha occasionally has reported something momentous, like the time she told me that the greatest thing about being a Christian is "knowing God's there with you all the time. I really feel him there."

That was something I've always prayed for.

Learning to pray short, ten-second prayers helps us learn to get out of the ruts. For instance, I used to pray at meals with a rote, "Thank you for today, Lord, and for this fine meal. Amen."

But a pastor friend of mine named David, who is the most amazing "quick prayer maker" I've ever encountered, inspired me to change this habit. His short prayers grip me and enclose me in a circle of power. Many times, as I've listened to him simply say grace at a meal, I've felt caught up to heaven in those few seconds, so eloquent and beautiful were his words. I wonder what God thought of my mantra at meals, every time, ad infinitum, ad nauseam. After listening to David, I've worked at learning to pray more reflectively, concisely, and simply. It works.

I'll admit, I used to get bored in prayer, just working to put in enough minutes to feel respectable. But God, I am convinced, wants us to learn to *enjoy* prayer, to make it such a fluid, beautiful part of our lives that we automatically avail ourselves of it in all situations. Enjoying prayer is far easier when we make it interesting, when we pray about varied subjects, and when we mix it up—using praise, thanks, and petition, in no special order, as thoughts and feelings occur to us.

As I was writing this chapter about the Creativity Principle, I thought of the creativity I use in my own prayer life and decided to put some of it into practice even as I worked. I told myself I'd pray every time I started a new paragraph. That became a fun way not only to take short breaks from the writing but to pray in the midst of it. For instance, I prayed after one paragraph that God would use this book to bless the people who read it. After the second paragraph, and taking a creative cue from the lyrics of an Amy Grant song, "Thy Word," playing on my computer, I asked God to help me enjoy, love, and steep my mind in his Word.

As I started this third paragraph, I prayed for my son and daughter, who had gone outside to play on our trampoline and then run around in the yard and spray each other with the hose. "Please help them not to get hurt, Father. And may they have a good time but not waste too much water."

You can use any spur you like in this kind of creative praying. Here are a few creative prayer jump-starts:

- any time the phone rings.

- every time you hear a dog bark.

- whenever you worry about money.

- every time you eat a piece of chocolate.

- each time you take a bite of your dinner.

- every time you switch from one program to another on your computer.

- each time you take a sip of coffee.

■ when you hear someone's raised voice. (Maybe even pray for that person.)

■ each time one of your kids asks you for something.

Things can get kind of comical when you pray like this, but that makes it fun. Of course, don't turn it into a legalistic thing. If you forget to pray, don't worry about it. Just pick up again with the next creative trigger.

You'll find that besides being fun, praying creatively helps improve your concentration and focus. And the best part is, it's a great way to stir up more prayer ideas in your heart and mind. I find that when I use creative methods like these, I often pray for the first thing that comes to mind. For instance, one of my articles appeared in the latest issue of *On Mission*, a Southern Baptist publication about evangelism and missions. The magazine lay on my desk by my computer for a while, and while I was offering a prayer every time I started a new paragraph in this chapter, one of those times I prayed that my article would have an impact and bless its readers.

A paragraph later, I noticed my checkbook. "Please work in the people at my bank, Lord, and give me an opportunity to plant some spiritual seeds there. I've often talked to Eva at the teller window, and I pray that you'll give me a chance to witness to her. And of course, give me lots of money to put into the bank account."

Okay, I didn't really add that last line, but I've been tempted.

Another paragraph, and I took a sip of my coffee, remembering that I'd gotten the beans at a local Sam's Club. "Jesus, bless Sam's Club, but help them not to put the Mom-and-Pop stores out of business."

Finally, when my daughter came to beg me to make her some popcorn, I prayed, "Lord, help me to finish this chapter with a flourish so I can go make that popcorn. Clearly, my daughter is starving."

Praying creatively like this can be fun, fulfilling, and even exciting. The Holy Spirit will teach you to pray like this if you ask. Why not stop right now and petition him to give you some new ideas about how to pray so your prayer life can become both powerful and fun!

CHAPTER THREE

THE THINGS-YOU-SEE-
ON-THE-WAY PRINCIPLE

On his way to work, Tom spotted people driving, walking their dogs, jogging, riding motorcycles, and one little guy pulling on his mom's arm as they stepped outside their home. As he passed each person, he prayed different things, like . . .

"Bless that person today and give him an opportunity to hear about you."

"Show that person something new and different and give her a day she'll remember."

"Help that person cheer and encourage someone in his family today."

And, "If I have a chance today, Lord, help

me to share the gospel with someone or simply plant a seed. Lead me."

Tom reached the main highway, and of course with so many people crowding in from all directions, he couldn't be as personal. He did not turn on the radio; he wanted to spend time in prayer and the music would distract him. So as he passed businesses, churches, and other buildings, he shot up several different types of prayer:

"Help that church to grow and lead people to Christ."

"Help that laundry business to prosper, Lord, and may they do a great job for their customers."

"Give that woman in the wheelchair the opportunity to know about you and have a blessed day today, Jesus."

And, "Help those schoolchildren bless their teachers today, Lord."

On the parkway a truck suddenly tore out from behind him, sped alongside, and quickly passed him, horn blaring all the way. Tom suddenly realized he'd been going a little slower than usual, so he sped up and said, "Give that truck driver a good day, and help him to be a little more patient with us slowpokes."

Of course, Tom didn't pray every minute of his commute. The drive to work was a good half hour, so he thought about things, prepared in his mind for a presentation he had to make later that day, and wrestled with other problems that came to mind.

The common denominator in all his thoughts, however, was the effortless, intermittent petitions he prayed in response to them as he drove. Every few minutes, as something occurred to him, he prayed about it. For instance, he remembered a situation that had developed between one of his coworkers and his secretary. Tom worried that an affair might develop, and as he thought about it, he prayed, "Lord, keep them from making a mistake. Guard them against sin and temptation."

That was it. Tom moved on to other things. But he genuinely hoped that one day his prayer efforts would be rewarded and he'd be privileged to see how the invisible, omnipotent God had worked in his world in response to such prayers. That became the hope to which Tom clung every day as he struggled to keep in touch with God through prayer: "Lord, show me what to pray about so I'm in tune with you, not just with my own thoughts and desires."

By the time he reached work, the heavy traffic had frazzled Tom a bit, so he sat in his car for an extra minute just to thank God for keeping him safe on the drive. Then he hurried into work, praying, as he always did, that God would bless his company, his team, and his coworkers.

On the way in he met up with Ken, a friend and co-worker to whom Tom had spoken several times about Christ. Tom shot another entreaty for Ken's salvation toward heaven.

"Have you heard what's going on?" Ken asked.

"No, what?"

"The progress report this quarter was bad. I've heard there might be layoffs."

Tom gulped and then prayed silently, "Jesus, if it does happen, help everyone land okay on this, please."

"I can't lose this job." Ken looked miserable and a little desperate.

Tom nodded. "I'll pray for you about it." He'd frequently mentioned praying about many things at the office to Ken, even though the man wasn't a Christian. Tom had often prayed for an opportunity to share his faith with Ken too.

Ken glanced warily at him. "Do you pray about everything, Tom?"

"Not everything. But lots of things."

"Why?"

Tom smiled. "Because it works. I see answers all the time."

"Like what?"

Tom thought for a second. "Remember when you told me you and your wife had argued and that you were afraid that when you got home she'd be gone?"

Ken nodded. "Boy, *do* I."

"She was home, right?"

"Yeah."

"And you made up, right?"

"Yeah."

"So I prayed for you—and for her."

Ken shrugged. "But wouldn't things have turned out that way even if you didn't pray?"

Tom shrugged. "Perhaps. But I wasn't willing to take that chance. So I asked God to get involved in your life. Just because rockets didn't go off doesn't mean God wasn't there or that he wasn't concerned.

God works in subtle ways most of the time, at least in my experience."

"Okay, then I guess I should thank you."

"I prayed about that too."

"About what?"

"That we'd get to talk about that incident and I'd have a chance to explain to you about prayer and God's concern for you."

"Really?"

"That was what—three months ago?"

"Yeah."

"Well, God answered that prayer today, right here."

"You're making me think this could be important, Tom."

"It is, Ken. Believe me, it is."

"Thanks."

Ken continued down the hall as Tom turned to enter his own office. "God, please allow my friendship with Ken to continue. Protect him and all my team—whatever happens."

He reached his desk and sat down, surveying the office, which reminded him of the possibility of layoffs.

He prayed again, "If there are layoffs, please help everyone to land safely somewhere."

The day hadn't started out well, but already Tom could tell his prayers were having an effect. In spite of the troubling rumors Tom had heard, his heart was at peace.

The more we recognize that prayer is a powerful response to any situation or circumstance, the more we'll pray. God wants us to be so aware of his presence in our lives that our conversation with him never ends. Sure, there'll be lulls and moments—even long periods—when we go silent. But if we remember that Jesus is right there with us, speaking to us about the needs around us and leading us to pray for specific needs and situations, we begin to see the world as our reminder, our road map, and our motivation to pray. We pray about anything that happens around us, events and situations we witness.

I believe the Spirit of God prompts us constantly about needs to pray for, people to talk to, openings to share our faith, and other opportunities we might otherwise overlook. He doesn't leave us out there in the world without an inner guide—his Spirit—leading us in the adventure God has planned for our lives.

What's more, the Bible promises that Christians will one day be rewarded for our deeds in the world. For instance, Paul writes in 2 Corinthians 5:10, "We must all appear before the judgment seat of Christ, so that each one may be recompensed for his deeds in the body, according to what he has done, whether good or bad." I believe prayer is a big part of that reward system. So the more prayers we offer up to God, the more occasions there will be for him to work in our midst—or even in places of the world we'll never physically go. When we pray only about our family, our church, or those things routinely on our minds, we overlook the many opportunities God has placed in our path on any given day. The more people, organizations, situations, and events we can pray for, the more God will work in the world. By the same token, the less we pray, the less he will work in us, in our lives, and in our communities.

I learned this principle early in my Christian life. I knew little about the Bible and even less about theology.

But I did know that Jesus was real and that he was with me wherever I went. I had learned a verse from Matthew 7:7 that said, "'Ask, and it will be given to you,'" and I took it seriously. I told myself to ask as much as possible, about everything. No concern was too small or too big for God to care about.

For instance, during my first winter as a Christian, I worked at a ski resort in Vermont. When I wasn't working, I skied. One of my friends from college also worked there, and at one point he found a deal where I could buy a new set of skis at nearly half price. I thought much about it. It looked like a good bargain. But then I asked God, "Should I do this?"

Soon I had my answer, and it was no. My present skis had many more years left in them, and the still small voice of the Spirit reminded me of that fact. I told my friend I would decline. He was angry with me, since he would have profited from this little business deal, but what could I do? I believed God had spoken.

As it turned out, after that winter I didn't have a chance to ski again for many years. Skiing enthusiast that I am, I had no idea that would happen. But God did.

Buying those skis would have been a waste of money. Perhaps that's why he said no to my short prayer.

It soon became natural and normal to include God in everything. "Lord, what do you want to teach me here?" Or, "Jesus, your world is so beautiful. Thank you for making it the greatest place to live in the universe." Or, "Father, please forgive me for that lie I told yesterday. Help me not to do that again." God was at my right hand, and no matter which way I turned, I found him like a beacon in the world, illuminating its needs and fears.

One day not too long ago, I felt a little depressed and prayed, "God, I need a few good laughs today. Please send some my way."

Later we went to church for Wednesday evening activities. While dropping off our youngest child at the nursery, I noticed someone had spilled the nametags onto the floor. I started to bend down to pick them up, but Gardner, my then seven-year-old, piped up, "I'll do it, Dad. I know you can't get down that far anymore."

I chuckled . . . and then I remembered my little prayer.

During the prayer meeting, a few jokes and cracks gave us some good laughs together as well.

And why not? Why wouldn't God care about such things? Do we need to wail and beg and pour out our hearts before God's throne? Sure, there's a time for that. But I think God honors short prayers as much as long ones. After all, when Peter tried walking on water to meet Jesus and started to sink, all he said was, "Lord, save me!" What more was needed? He certainly couldn't skip over to his prayer closet and cry out in secret.

If we can get hold of this idea of praying without ceasing, we will have found a tool that can help us face any difficulty we encounter in this world with God's victory. Nothing's wrong with listening to music to relax us as we drive home, but using the time to pray for the people we see on the way, in their cars, or at stoplights, makes life an adventure instead of a dull drag through town each morning.

Think of every person you see—every business, every church—as subjects for prayer. When you have that frame of mind, heaven will move in your world. And as a result, you'll become a force for change in your community.

CHAPTER FOUR

THE LISTEN-FOR-
THE-SPIRIT'S-PROMPTING
PRINCIPLE

At the office Tom concentrated on the work at hand. But some situations still called for prayer. For instance, his computer suddenly began acting up, and he didn't know why. The company didn't employ someone dedicated to fixing such problems, so if Tom wanted to continue working, he would have to try to solve it on his own, checking with coworkers or, if he was really stumped, calling an outside technician for guidance. But a still, small voice spoke to his mind: "Pray about this." So he did. "Lord, I know I'm missing something here. Please show me what it is so I can fix this problem and get on with my work."

He opened his computer manual and paged through it. He rebooted and performed all the basic steps prescribed for troubleshooting. Then, out of the blue, he saw what the problem was. It felt beyond him—as if God had stuck his finger right on the page and said, "Here's your problem." With a quick prayer of praise, Tom fixed the problem and got back to work.

At lunchtime Tom went out to eat with several co-workers. They had a good time. But as they ate, Tom mentioned each one to God by name as someone he'd like to share his faith with, asking God for an open door or for someone else to speak to them about the love of the Lord. Tom prayed for the waitress, for the owner of the restaurant, and for its success in the community. He didn't machine-gun God with a steady barrage of requests, but in quiet moments when his mind became aware of a need or opportunity, he turned the thought into a quick prayer. He joked along with his friends, but he also communicated to God his concerns for each of them.

Although Tom had caught a ride to the restaurant

with Luis, he would need to ride back with someone else, as Luis had to leave early. So when Tom noticed Jeff walking to his car alone, looking discouraged, he sensed that this might be an opportunity prompted by the Spirit. "Hey Jeff," he called out. "Mind if I ride with you?" If God were planning this road trip, he'd gladly ride along.

Tom had been praying about Jeff for a while, fearing he might be having an affair with an attractive woman in their office. This would give the two men a chance to talk privately. Was God working in response to Tom's earlier prayers? The silence felt awkward, and Tom prayed, "Lord, please lead me to say and do the right things right now. Work in Jeff's heart. Prepare him to hear and accept your truth."

"I'm having a real problem, Tom," Jeff blurted out, much to Tom's amazement. Jeff didn't even notice Tom's speechless shock, but continued. "I know you're a Christian, and I'd like you to pray about something for me."

Jeff revealed his fear that his wife might be having an affair. Tom listened carefully but continued praying for God's wisdom and help while Jeff talked.

Tom hesitated to ask the tough question that was in

his mind, but again he felt the Spirit speak to his heart: "Go ahead, ask him."

"I've noticed you talking to Erin a lot lately," Tom said cautiously. "Were you asking her advice or something?"

Jeff nodded. "Erin's pretty open and easy to talk to, so I've been asking her about the signs of an affair. Remember, her husband had one a few years ago. They divorced. Erin encouraged me to confront Chloe, and then, if it's true and she'll stop the affair, to forgive her."

Tom had prayed about Erin's marital troubles a while back too. Unfortunately, God hadn't answered that prayer the way Tom had hoped. But he also had prayed for Erin's spiritual growth and renewal in the midst of that difficult time, and this seemed like evidence of that happening.

Jeff parked the car and continued, obviously distraught. "I love Chloe. She's the only one who has ever really believed in me." He pounded his fist on the steering wheel. "But now it looks like she's started believing more in some other guy. It hurts."

Jeff looked away, clearly upset, and Tom felt the Spirit prompting him to pray for his friend out loud. "Jeff," he asked, "can I pray for you about this right now?"

Jeff shrugged. "Do you think it could help?"

Tom responded, "I know God can help you. Let me just take a minute now and pray."

When they finished praying, Jeff said, "Thanks. I really feel better. You know, I was supposed to go out with Dave, but he backed out at the last minute so I decided to drive over and join you guys. But this was good. Things turned out better than I could have planned them."

Because God planned them, Tom thought with satisfaction, adding silently, "Thank You, God, for allowing me to be part of your plan."

When we respond to God's promptings to pray, we'll find ourselves praying about numerous subjects we might never think of on our own. Sure, God can bring to mind people who have needs at regularly scheduled prayer times, but why hold the prayer response in check until we can be alone and quiet? Why not respond to the stimulus the Spirit of God puts in our minds? Why not pray immediately about a need that has come up, instead of promising to do so at night before bed or some other quiet time?

I've found it's great to pray for a person right as he or she tells me about a need. For instance, when Tom talked to Jeff, he didn't wait. He prayed right there—in his mind—as Jeff talked. That way he didn't have to worry he might forget later. We multitask in everything else, why not prayer? Our minds are capable of praying as we listen to someone's situation and even as we talk ourselves. Besides, offering to pray out loud for someone is also a great way to encourage that person and to show we care. It may even plant in people's minds seeds of interest in God and faith. How do we expect people to know that God has answered prayer on their behalf if they don't even know someone's praying? And what do we think will draw them to want to get to know God as we do if we don't even demonstrate our reliance on God by turning to him when we have needs and talking to him as we would to a friend?

My friend Paul felt the Holy Spirit's prompting one night as he balanced his checkbook. He had a thousand extra dollars, and he wondered if God wanted him to do something special with it. Almost immediately God answered and sent him to a friend who ministered to poor people. When Paul offered the check, the friend's voice broke with obvious emotion as he explained that he'd been asking God what to do about a shortfall in his budget for that week—a shortfall of precisely a thousand dollars.

Paul went away rejoicing not only because his money would be put to good use but because he'd been sensitive to the Spirit's leading so God could use him to bless a ministry and a servant of God in need. Isn't that the essence of ministering in the here and now?

I'll never forget the feeling I had when God used me in a similar way—urging me to go out of my way to do something that was his idea, not mine. I had been driving around running errands when an idea registered in my mind: *Go by Linda Miller's house.*

Linda was a member of my congregation who often requested prayer for her father, who was not a believer. Her mother, Frieda, also attended our church and had mentioned many times that her husband, Frank, needed prayer regarding his drinking and other problems. I'd visited Frieda before but never met Frank. I think he stayed away from me on purpose.

Pressed for time and thinking it was just a random thought popping into my head, I brushed it off. But the Spirit didn't let me go that easily. He kept prompting me to do something concerning Linda. I didn't know what it was, but a little more insistently, the thought reappeared: *Stop by Linda's.*

"Come on," I protested. "I don't have time, and it's late." It was past eight, and dropping by unannounced on a Saturday evening was not something I'd like someone to do to me.

The prodding wouldn't subside, though, and finally I gave in and drove toward Linda's house.

When I knocked on the door, Linda's mother answered. Frieda stared at me, sighed with relief, and said, "I've been trying to reach you for hours, Mark. It's Frank."

I thought it might be a heart attack or some such emergency, but it wasn't. This was a different kind of heart problem. Frank was struggling with feelings he'd never experienced before.

Baseball cap on his head, stubble on his chin, alcohol

on his breath, Frank greeted me warmly. But when I sat down, he couldn't speak. Several times he looked up and said, "I . . ." But he couldn't finish.

Frieda touched his hand affectionately. "It's okay, Frank. Just tell him what's on your mind."

Finally he got it out. "I'm a screwup, Mark . . . and I'm scared . . . real scared."

"Of what?" I asked.

He took a long breath. "That I'm going to die like this, a drinker who never did his family right. That it's too late. That I can't change now. That it's over for me."

"It's never too late, Frank," I said gently.

I told him about the thief on the cross. Frank said he remembered that story, and I said, "If it wasn't too late for him, it can't be too late for you."

Frank shook his head. "But you don't know what I've done."

This time I shook my head. "But God does know. Look at how he's worked things out tonight. Here Frieda's been trying to call me for hours, and then suddenly I just show up here, not even at your house. God knew how to get me here. He knew what was on your heart. He's reaching out to you. I'm convinced of that, Frank. What other reason could there be?"

Frank's eyes locked with my own in spiritual struggle. "But I just don't see how he could accept me . . . the way I am . . . the way I've been."

"But he does," I said quietly. "Frank, God knows everything you've ever done, the good *and* the bad. It doesn't matter anymore. He only asks that you accept the gifts he offers in Jesus—salvation, eternal life, forgiveness, spiritual power—all of it's free, and it can all be yours right now if you'll just trust him."

He blinked, and his eyes filled with tears. "I want to," he rasped. "I want to belong to him. I want this to be settled. Will he really take me?"

We knelt there in the living room and prayed. First, I prayed, then Frank. "God," he said, "I've screwed everything up. Everything. Please help me stop drinking. And help me get my life straightened out. And help me to love people the way I should. And be my Lord and Savior. That's all I ask."

Tears burned in my eyes as I listened. It was a jolt, one of those grand moments of grace and peace that come when we help someone find God.

Over the years Frank became one of the most accepting and loving people in our church. What God had done for him, he passed on to others.

I wonder, though, what might have happened had I not heeded God's nudge in my heart. Would the moment have passed? Would Frank have forgotten his conviction? Would he have despaired and given up on ever turning to God?

I know, of course, that if God wanted to help Frank, God would do so even if I failed in my part of the mission. God is not unfaithful, even if we sometimes are.

But I would have missed being part of the faith-affirming process of leading Frank to Christ. I would have missed an opportunity to see firsthand the powerful effect of prayer. I would have missed that joy that comes from knowing God hears, speaks to, and uses us. I simply would not have been there. And for me, that would have been a real loss.

I believe God works in many ways, but I also believe there are moments when a heart is most ready to receive God. His Spirit speaks to us in those moments and moves us to action—sometimes action we might consider odd or unwarranted. We put ourselves on the line when we follow the Spirit's prompting to act. What if we're wrong and that thought isn't God but rather our own inner voice? Aren't we presumptuous to think God is speaking to us? What if the other person misses God's signals?

But that's not our responsibility. We're responsible only for our own actions. When God calls us to act, we must step out in faith.

Don't you love being prompted by the Spirit? It seems he's always whispering something in my brain, and when I follow his lead, I get to be part of the solution to a real problem.

Listen. Respond. Pray. Then watch God work.

CHAPTER FIVE

THE MEDIA PRINCIPLE

As Tom waited for his coffee to finish brewing in the break room, he sat and read the newspaper. On the front page of the local section, he read with interest an unbelievable account of a young woman who'd botched a crime so badly that she could easily win one of those competitions for most stupid criminal. It was the kind of story that not only made a person smile and scratch his head in bemusement but practically begged to be retold around the water cooler or dinner table. It took a while for Tom's usual instincts to kick in and make him think to pray for this troubled young woman. "Lord, I don't know what drove her to this, but please speak to her. Minister to her and help her find a way out of her darkness."

The coffeemaker beeped, signaling that Tom's wait was over. But before he could react and move toward it, Betty, Jeff's secretary, was there. She must have heard it too and breezed into the room, passing Tom on her way to the coffee. But she stopped short beside Tom, making noises of surprise and then compassion. "Oh, wow, you've seen the article? Isn't that something?"

Tom nodded, a faint smile on his face. "The only thing more embarrassing than being in the newspaper for breaking the law might be getting in the paper for being such an inept criminal."

"That's Bill's stepdaughter," Betty whispered.

"Bill?"

"In shipping. He's totally broken up about it."

"Wow," Tom said, shocked. "I guess he would be."

The realization that he was somehow connected to a person in the news rattled Tom a little and changed his perspective. This was not some cardboard cutout for people to laugh at or scorn. She was a living, breathing person—someone's daughter, sister, friend. He felt immense empathy for Bill. For the first time, Tom could imagine the anguish endured by the families of a much-criticized politician, an executive mired in scandal, or a celebrity whose drunk-driving mug shot was splashed across every media outlet around the world. In that moment, people in the news seemed more real to Tom than ever before, and he recognized in a fresh, new way the importance of praying for them.

Although Tom had often used what he read in newspapers and magazines or what he saw on the television news as prompts to pray for people and situations, the incident with Bill's stepdaughter made his effort more personal and determined. His prayers for these people and their families seemed crucial: They were real people with real feelings and needs. Their actions or situations impacted many lives beyond their own. He could only begin to imagine the hidden ripple effect of each news item— and each prayer he prayed.

Most of us read magazines and consult the news each day, even if it's via the Internet. This is a perfect time to pray for the needs raised in those articles. Do you believe prayer has spiritual, economic, personal, and physical power? Does God refuse to act in our world if we don't pray?

Luke 18:1 says that Jesus told his disciples a parable "to show that at all times they ought to pray and not to lose heart." It's clear Jesus is saying we shouldn't "faint" or "give up," even when we don't seem to see immediate answers to our prayers. If the woman in Jesus's parable had given up on her second, third, or fourth petition of the unjust judge, she would have stopped just short of receiving the answer she sought. How many Christians give up one prayer short of seeing God's answer? When we cease praying, we abandon our stake in the process. Perhaps God will not work as we might have seen him do had we pressed on. Perhaps he will not act on behalf of the people who desperately need it. In the book of Judges, when the people of Israel forgot God and didn't pray, everything in their lives and in their nation went haywire. But when they turned back to God, he sent good leaders who led them out of their troubles.

The Bible teaches consistently that when we pray, God works in the world. What truth could better motivate us to prayer? And the more I pray about items I see or hear in the news, the more I'm convinced that prayer works.

In the 2004 presidential campaign between John Kerry and George W. Bush, I entered the race myself by praying about these men's integrity, ideas, and work. When the Swift Boat Veterans for Truth charges against Kerry appeared in the media, I prayed that the truth of the matter would be revealed and that God would give each American citizen discernment to choose wisely when casting a vote for president.

Over the years I've taken my cues from the media to pray about the following people and events:

- the abduction and recovery of the Utah teenager, Elizabeth Smart;

- the release and success of *Let's Roll!* (Lisa Beamer's book about her husband, Todd, who was on Flight 93 when it crashed in Pennsylvania on 9/11);

- upon the death of George Harrison of the Beatles, that the remaining Beatles would be drawn to God for comfort.

- Mel Gibson's movie *The Passion of the Christ*— for its success and that it would have a positive influence on all who viewed it;

- that the influence of various books by atheists Sam Harris and Richard Dawkins would be minimal and that their arguments would be soundly refuted; and

- for Indianapolis Colts head coach Tony Dungy, whom I heard was a Christian—that his success would bring media exposure that would enable him to share his faith with the world.

I'm not claiming that things worked out the way they did because I prayed. I'm sure millions of Christians stormed the throne of God about the presidential election. I don't believe God is a Republican, Democrat, or Independent; a liberal, conservative, or centrist. My candidates haven't always won, and I think many winning candidates clearly had no interest in promoting God's kingdom or truth. But God does give us wisdom and discernment if we ask him, and he reassures us that he's in control. Daniel 2:21–22 ties it all together when it says of God: "He removes kings and establishes kings; He gives wisdom to wise men and knowledge to men of understanding. It is He who reveals the profound and hidden things; He knows what is in the darkness, and the light dwells with Him."

If Christians want to be politically involved in the world, even without working in someone's campaign or making financial contributions, what better way than to pray? Why shouldn't we think God will work in our nation and in our own hearts, leading and guiding us as individuals and as a country as elections unfold?

Some will say, "But what about all the Christians who pray and come to opposite conclusions on a candidate or issue?"

The body of Christ has room for different political preferences and opinions. It's important to remember that a person's spirituality or salvation doesn't rise or fall on where he or she stands in the political spectrum. The reasons we support or oppose a party or candidate are complex and varied. As long as we all seek God, try to discern and follow his leading, and always subordinate our wishes to his sovereignty, Christians should have no trouble praying together about political issues—and getting along while doing it. Prayers like, "May your will be done, God"; "Lead our nation in your path, Lord"; and, "Give us discernment about the candidates and issues" are petitions we can offer in unity.

Ultimately I believe we should pray about the spiritual elements of such things, not the political results. Thus, we can pray for things such as

- the salvation or spiritual growth of various candidates;

- that the truth will come out;

- that God's will be done and his kingdom come, and that we as praying Christians will see his work in the midst of it;

- that the people in politics will gain real interest in the spiritual elements of their actions and policies (helping people in need, etc.);

■ that God will prevent evil people from gaining power and doing evil things, but that if such things do happen, God will use it, in the end, for his glory and the good of his people.

Over the past few years I've become more and more interested in world events and prayed for many situations I've learned about through media reports. The tsunami that struck the Pacific Rim nations at the end of 2004 and Hurricane Katrina in 2005 particularly inspired me to pray for the people whose lives the storms had devastated. Shortly after both of these events, my church sent teams of nurses, doctors, and aid workers to minister to affected people in those places. I knew many of the members involved and prayed for them specifically.

Once more event that has caught my attention on the world scene is the war in Iraq. I pray repeatedly about the military campaign there and the soldiers fighting in it, as well as for the recovery and rehabilitation of Iraq and the many devastated civilians and soldiers. As al Qaeda in Iraqi insurgent leader Abu Musab al-Zarqawi's increasingly bloody attacks continued making news, I began beseeching God to work to change the man's beliefs and undermine his influence. As everyone knows, one day we all awoke to learn he'd been killed.

Do I honestly think my prayers had any effect on the events I've mentioned?

As I read the Bible, I repeatedly see accounts of the power of prayer—from Moses talking God out of annihilating the idol-worshipping Israelites in Exodus 32:7–14 to Abraham praying on behalf of Sodom and Gomorrah in Genesis 18:22–33 to Hezekiah's prayer for healing in 2 Kings 20:1–6 and other astonishing answers from God to his praying people.

If the Bible teaches anything, it's that God responds to our faith and our prayers and acts on our behalf. Why would God show us repeatedly the influence faithful people had through prayer and then deny us in the twenty-first century the same power and privilege? On the contrary, Paul wrote in Romans 15:4, "Whatever was written in earlier times was written for our instruction, so that through perseverance and the encouragement of the Scriptures we might have hope." That hope includes the belief that when we pray, God will take action on our behalf and on behalf of the world.

Every election cycle, I read in some pundit's column about how if one vote had changed in a precinct here and a precinct there, a national election's outcome might have been changed. What about prayer? Is it possible that when many people are praying about an issue that one person's entreaty could tip the balance and cause God to move? Of course, God is sovereign. But he does respond to his people. Could your prayer be the one that moves him to action?

We know from the Bible that many times one person's prayers moved God to tremendous action. In 1 Kings 17 we read that Elijah told King Ahab it wouldn't rain in Israel so long as Elijah prayed against it. And it didn't rain until he prayed that it would—three years later.

In 1 Samuel 1 we find Hannah beseeching God to give her a son. Her prayer was answered, and Samuel was born—a baby who would grow up to be one of the greatest prophets and judges of Israel.

In Job 42, at the end of the drama and Job's testing, God told him to pray for his three "friends," the heartless advisors who had counseled Job so badly in his time of despair and affliction. God forgave them on the basis of Job's prayers.

In 2 Kings 19:8–20 and 32–37 we find the history of how God defeated the mighty armies of Sennacherib at the gates of Jerusalem because King Hezekiah prayed. Even Herodotus, the great Greek historian, acknowledged this miraculous victory, although he attributed the victory to a rodent-borne plague that decimated the Assyrian army.

Over and over I hear from Christians who don't want to "waste their lives in trivia." They don't want to be nonplayers on the world stage. They long for significance, a sense of being part of something bigger than themselves, and feeling that what they do in their lives really matters. Few of us can end poverty, bring about peace in the Middle East, extinguish bigotry and racism, or stop a nuclear holocaust. Even the president of the United States and other world leaders often have been unable to accomplish lasting and positive changes of such magnitude.

But we don't have to be political dignitaries to tap

into unlimited, almighty power. Through prayer we can influence the real hand of power to shape world events. Since God is the answer, and prayer moves the hand of God, will you resolve to make prayer a bigger priority in your life starting right now?

CHAPTER SIX

THE SHIFT PRINCIPLE

Prayer can become boring and repetitive if you don't work at it. It's easy to slip into the groove of praying the same things for your family, yourself, and others. It takes discipline and some work to stay out of a prayer rut.

That's why Tom often used something in his prayer life he called "the shift." In this system he told himself something like, "For the next few hours, I will pray only about my co-workers." From that point on, every time the Spirit of God brought a coworker to mind, he would pray for that person. Often it was a general prayer: "Please bless this person today, and help him get his work done with speed and skill." Or, "Lord, encourage her today some-

how—perhaps through something that crosses her desk."
Or, "God, as you said in Hebrews 4:12, your word is
'living and active and sharper than any two-edged sword.'
Use your word to convict Joe of any wrongdoing and
draw him back to you."

Sometimes Tom got even more specific. He singled
out coworkers with special needs and concerns—Jeff, who
was worried about his marriage; Bill, from shipping, and
his wayward stepdaughter; Ken, who was terrified he'd
lose his job—and made each one the exclusive subject of
a prayer shift. He started with Jeff. Whenever he had a
moment, Tom prayed that he'd get the opportunity to talk
to Jeff about God; that Jeff's marriage would be saved;
and that Tom would be a source of encouragement to
him.

Then, after an hour or so of focusing on Jeff, Tom's
next prayer shift would focus to Ken and the job situation. After praying for Ken numerous times in the following hour, he moved on to focusing on Bill and his
stepdaughter: that God would work good out of the
situation, that Tom would be a comfort and help to
Bill's family, and that God would speak to the young

woman and make her want God's help to turn her life around.

After a while of praying for various coworkers, Tom would shift his focus in a more major way. "Okay, now I'm going to pray strictly for people and events in my community and world whenever the Spirit calls them to mind." If he read or heard any news in that timeframe, he would pray about that particular situation: "God, work in the aftermath of the earthquake in Indonesia. Speed food and assistance to the survivors." And, "Jesus, be with the people in that accident I heard about on the radio traffic report. Help any who are hurt to get to a hospital and get the treatment they need." And, "Father, please help this hurricane season to be light. Protect people's lives and property. If storms do hit, may the response be quick and efficient."

For the two hours Tom focused on situations in the world around him, he prayed for a wide variety of issues and needs. Then, at the end of the time he had allotted, he would shift again: "Now I'll pray only for people in my community." For that time period he would call out to God on behalf of people he knew who did not know

Christ or who had some other specific need. "Help our next-door neighbors, Lord. They're getting old and finding it difficult to keep up their home and yard. I don't know if they know you. Give me an opportunity to be a blessing and help to them as well as be a witness." And, "You know the situation with the family across the street that is moving because of a divorce. Lord, if it's your will, help them find reconciliation of some sort. Protect the kids at this difficult time. Work good in your own way and timing."

At the end of the day, when Tom looked back at where his praying "shifts" had taken him, he realized he'd covered vast and unique territories: around the globe, around the neighborhood, and down endless avenues of need and opportunity.

The shift is an easy method to use in prayer, and it keeps you from praying the same old stuff all the time. It gives you a creative way to touch on many different people and different parts of the community.

Below are just some of the subjects you can shift to during the day.

- family and friends

- extended family

- the government

- the War on Terror

- Afghanistan and Iraq

- Muslims

- neighbors

- your church

- your small group

- your job and coworkers

- your city

- your children's teachers and classmates

- your upcoming vacation

- moral issues

- upcoming legislation

- the courts and criminal justice system

You can see how this process would encourage you to focus on many different issues and subjects you might not normally consider. Instead of traveling the same ruts day in and day out, you can impact the heart of our world, covering many different subjects and issues and the people they affect.

I don't use the shift every day. But it's a good method for when you're too tired to pray through a Scripture passage or you want to explore new territory for the kingdom of God. Go a little wild with this. Make up your own categories, and get as original and creative as you like. Anything will do, but strive to choose categories that lend themselves to multiple points of departure.

One of my favorite examples is when I select the major topic of praying for the many people I've known in my life. Since I've lived in lots of places, I usually divide the shift by place and time. Thus, I'll pray:

- for people I knew in my early years in Lansdale, Pennsylvania;

- then for my friends in Cherry Hill, New Jersey, where I lived from the age of eight until I was twenty-one;

- next for those I knew in college;

- then on to students I crossed paths with in seminary;

- and so on, through all the places and eras of my life right up to the present.

This way I consciously remind myself to pray for people I might never even think of, let alone pray for, otherwise — many of whom I haven't seen for years. It doesn't have to be specific or take long. I might not even know their life situation, but God knows. And even without knowing many details, I find plenty to pray about.

"Lord, help my friend Dusty to find you."

"Jesus, open Freddy's heart to your truth."

"Father, speak to my friends from Colgate U."

In fact, I've prayed many times for the people I knew in college. Every now and then I hear from someone who has come across one of my books. As a result, I've been able to talk to many of them about God, and in some cases I believe significant seeds of faith have been planted in their hearts. So now I pray specifically that each one will come to fruition in God's good time.

The Shift Principle gives me occasion to pray for many people who are beyond the usual scope of my prayers. Even when no immediate fruit results from my conversations with the people from my past whom I've prayed for, I truly believe the positive contacts and opportunities to share what God is doing in my life all have resulted from my prayers over the years—prayers for these people's lives, souls, and happiness.

The Shift Principle can help you cover a lot of ground in your prayer life too. Don't just mouth the same prayers all the time. Be adventurous. It might get you praying and involved in the work of the kingdom of God in ways you never dreamed possible.

CHAPTER SEVEN

THE LISTS PRINCIPLE

Tom loved walking. It was a good way to get in some exercise, see the sights, and meet his neighbors. It was also a great way to do some praying.

As he passed houses, he prayed for the people who lived there, even if he didn't know them. The beauty of walking was that it became a way to make contacts and start conversations about God in addition to praying for his neighbors as he passed by. His exercise regimen required that he walk at least a half hour four days a week. So that allowed him to log nearly two hours of prayer weekly. It was easy. When his mind wandered to some problem or concern, he reminded himself to pray about it rather than wasting the time worrying.

At times the spontaneous nature of ten-second praying felt disorganized. Sure, it was great for praying for things that easily came to mind. But what about some of the pressing situations that happened day by day and week by week that needed his attention, even if they weren't things he remembered often?

That dilemma led Tom to the old prayer warrior's practice of keeping lists. He simply jotted down on sheets of paper the names of people, situations, and events that needed prayer and then used these as prompts for ten-second prayers of many sorts. On any one list, he might run through ten or twenty situations, calling out to God to intervene. Tom gave each item on the list a ten-second prayer and then moved on. It wasn't unusual for long silences to separate each prayer, but eventually he would go back to the list and pick up where he'd left off.

Tom carried other kinds of lists as he walked too. Each morning he made up a to-do list of activities he wanted to tackle that day. If he walked at lunchtime, he would pray about his to-do list. Once a week he updated the list, crossed off items he knew were no longer timely or necessary, and prayed about each new request he'd become aware of and added to the list.

The prayer lists weren't hard to keep organized. Tom put them in his wallet or pocket so he could pull them out whenever he was ready to use them. Usually he prayed through each list once and then moved on. This way, praying by lists never became tedious or boring, because he always had new lists with new prayer requests. Although Tom prayed only about ten seconds for each need, by the end of his walk or the end of the week, he ended up logging many minutes in prayer through this method.

When Tom ate breakfast with his family, they often shared their prayer requests. One morning the concerns included several things:

- Some kids were making fun of Brad because he prayed before eating his lunch.

- Ginny needed God's help to do her best on a difficult test.

- Their elderly dog, Jody, was declining. Perhaps God would touch her and give her strength and renewed health. They needed God's wisdom and grace to deal with the situation and make good decisions.

■ Tom's work situation was becoming more difficult and less certain. That was always on his list, but perhaps the kids would add it to theirs.

Tom quickly added the new items to his prayer list, put it in his pocket, and headed to work. There he laid the list on his desk to remind him to pray about those needs during the day. At one point Erin came by to pick up a report and noticed the list.

"What's that, Tom?" she asked, obviously curious. "Troubles at home?"

"No, just things I'm praying for. The kids had some things on their hearts, and so did Darla. I make a list so I won't forget to pray."

"You really believe in prayer, don't you?" Erin asked. She seemed to be testing the waters, but he couldn't tell if she approved or disapproved of his praying.

"God's done a lot of incredible things in my life," he answered.

"Tell me one."

Tom told her about how he had prayed for Bill, in shipping, and his troubled stepdaughter and then had gotten to talk with Bill several times. "He's given his heart and life to Christ since then. It has changed his life—and his daughter is doing better. Her trial is coming up, and her lawyer thinks he can get the judge to show leniency because she's a first-time offender with a good chance of turning her life around."

"Wow. That really is something."

"It's always a thrill to see God working on behalf of someone I've prayed about."

Erin stood there, nodding, then averted her gaze as tears began to form. "Would you put me on your list? Please. Just for a few days."

"Of course," Tom said, his concern evident. "What's wrong, Erin? I'll pray for it as long as it takes."

She walked over to the chair and sat down, her makeup slightly smeared. "My mom is dying of cancer. Not much time left, I think."

She stopped and wiped her eyes angrily. "I hate crying. I hate it."

"It's okay," Tom said and handed her a tissue.

Erin took a deep breath. "My mom's my best friend in all the world, and I don't know how I'll live without her. But I don't know what to do. And the doctors—" She sniffled again. "The doctors don't offer any hope. So I guess it's just gonna happen." She blew her nose and looked at Tom. "It's just so hard."

Tom was sympathetically quiet a moment, then asked, "What would you like me to pray?"

She looked away and cocked her head thoughtfully. "I don't know. I don't know anything about God, prayer, or any of that. I went to church as a kid, but you know how those things are. All my life, I've just tried to survive. But I don't know what to do anymore."

Erin released a frustrated sigh, then asked, "So what would you pray for me?"

Tom thought about it. "Okay," he said as the Spirit seemed to fill his mind with ideas. "First of all, you'll be on my list for as long as this takes. I'll remember to pray every day. I'll ask God to heal your mother or at least slow the cancer's advance. I know God can heal, but he doesn't always. So I'll ask that if it's your mother's time to go, God will be with her every step of the way: that he'll take her gently and lovingly, and that she—and you—will be able to get things in order before that time, spiritually and in your relationship."

Wide-eyed, Erin nodded and seemed to agree with what Tom was saying. She smiled, blew her nose, and said, "Tom, I don't know if I really believe that prayer can do all you believe it does, but I sure hope so. Guess I'll find out."

"Guess so," Tom said kindly, confidently. "I guess so."

I often see people on the street or sidewalk, speeding by in their "power walk" with headphones on, listening to music or audiobooks. They look like they're in pain as they rip by, and I'm glad my walks don't require that I turn myself into a machine. A leisurely walk can be good exercise, but it's also a great time to talk to God. Frankly, I recommend walking and praying to anyone who likes the idea of killing two birds with one stone.

But walking isn't the only good way to pray through a

list. During breaks at work, during lunch while you're munching on your tuna salad, and a million other times are moments when you can turn to your list and zing those requests to God.

A friend of mine puts prayer requests on tape. He records a request, then leaves a blank space of ten to fifteen seconds to give himself time to pray about each request before moving on to the next one. Then, when he goes walking or driving in his car, he pops in the tape and responds to the prompts by praying for the many different needs.

I often take prayer lists to the local Sam's Club and pray while I make my way through this huge store. I find it interesting to walk down aisle after aisle just to see what's available. Sometimes I take my two little ones with me—Gardner, who was eight, loves to look at the video games, and Elizabeth, who was two, points out all the things she likes as we walk along. "Barney!" she'll cry, and, "Scooby-Doo!"

On one of the walk-and-pray excursions I shared with my kids, Gardner was having a tough time with all of the abundance around him. Seeing the rows of video games reminded him of his lost Game Boy, which my wife had bought for him on eBay as a special gift.

A week or so earlier, he had fallen asleep on the couch in our family room. When he awoke later, the Game Boy was gone. Of course, everyone thought two-year-old Elizabeth had heisted it. But she denied this. (At least it sounded like a denial; it was mostly shakes of the head and intermittent no's and yeses to our various questions.) The upshot was that she couldn't tell us what—if anything—she'd done with it. After it had been missing for several days, I told Gardner to start praying about it. His sad bemoaning of the fact that he no longer had a machine to play his games on made me move him and the missing Game Boy to the top of the prayer list in my pocket. "Please, Lord, help us to find that Game Boy," I'd often pray. "And teach Gardner some important lessons through this."

I worried that we had inadvertently thrown away the Game Boy. But I kept the problem before the Lord, and he seemed to reassure me not to stop praying about it, a kind of prompt I often feel when God signals that something will receive a yes from him.

More than a week passed, and although the Game Boy was still a matter of prayer, it was no longer at the top of my list. Then one day Gardner ran to find me, obviously excited. "Elizabeth found my Game Boy!" he cried.

"What?" I asked, delighted and amazed. "Where?"

We went to Elizabeth, but she just shook her head. She didn't seem to know what we meant as we asked, "Where did you find the Game Boy, Elizabeth?" Finally, she pointed to a trash can. It was one we keep in our family room, and since it doesn't fill up too quickly, it had not been emptied in a couple of weeks. How easily we might have emptied it, unaware of the treasure it contained, and that expensive Game Boy would have been gone forever.

But God knew about our problem. Though it took two weeks, he still answered. "God answered our prayer, didn't he, Dad?" Gardner said.

"He sure did."

"From now on, I'm going to pray about everything," Gardner said. "No matter what it is, I'm praying about it."

"Like what?"

"Like that I never lose my Game Boy again."

"Great idea. Anything else?"

"That you'll buy me a box of ice cream bars."

I chuckled, but I think his attitude is great. Our kids will catch our vision for prayer if we include them in our prayer times.

Here are some ideas about the kinds of lists you can use to get you praying:

- A list of personal needs. Simply list the things you're concerned about—your family, your work, your church, etc.

- Prayer lists you get at church. Some churches hand these out at midweek services; others provide them in the bulletin or online. They often include notices about church members or extended families in the hospital, in grief, or with special needs. Find these flyers in your church and use them. Just don't feel locked into praying about these things over and over. God assures us he hears every prayer, even those we utter only once.

- Lists from missions organizations and other parachurch groups. If you're like me, you get many e-mails and mailings each week from missionaries and others who mention their particular needs. Interceding right when I get the letters may not be the most timely or the best approach, so I often take these lists on my walks and pray about them.

- Special lists you may keep for your walk. (We'll talk more about this in chapter 15, on using a prayer cycle.) This is an excellent way to pray about many needs and people in the world and in your life.

- Bible verses you want to pray through. (More about this in chapter 11, on praying the Scriptures).

- Running lists. Anything you use to keep up with needs and that you can adjust by adding new requests or deleting those that have been answered.

I use various kinds of lists, not only to keep my prayer time fresh and interesting, but also to keep abreast of what's going on in my church community. One list that's important to me is the list our group puts together each time we gather for our church prayer meeting. We pass a piece of paper around the circle, and everyone writes down any prayer need they have that's urgent or pressing. One person then makes and distributes copies for each member so we all can take them home and continue praying about those needs. I pray through the whole list at least once. It's exciting to know that many other people are praying for those same needs, and it's especially rewarding when we see the results of our prayers.

One woman mentioned that her brother's grandson had developed a serious skin disease that could end his life at an early age. Her brother, who wasn't a Christian, was understandably distraught. We prayed. Several weeks later she reported that doctors said the disease had "strangely gone into remission" and the boy was free of it completely. She said her brother also was asking new questions about prayer and faith.

Another member spoke of a problem regarding custody of her daughter's three children, who were in foster care. "We're willing to take the kids ourselves," she said, "but the state won't let us. We need to get God involved so they'll let us bring the kids home." It was a heartrending situation, and we all gathered around beseeching God to intervene. A few months after praying, the woman happily reported, "We have the kids. They released them to us this week." We all rejoiced.

One of our members had to undergo knee replacement surgery. He was worried and a little frightened that he might not be able to walk again, so we prayed. Today this man not only walks but has a healthy spring in his step.

And I've benefited from being on the group's prayer list as well. One week I was rather upset about our new cat, Frodo. My wife and kids were in Texas visiting Granny, but I'd had to stay home. One night Frodo got out and disappeared. I didn't see him for days. I didn't want to tell Jeanette about it because Frodo was her favorite pet (we have two hamsters, two dogs, two cats, and two fish), but finally I fessed up. Jeanette insisted I call for Frodo and look for him all over the yard, because he might be hiding from the dog. I did, but I still could find neither hide nor whiskers of him anywhere.

Finally I shared the kitty crisis at the prayer meeting and put it on our list. Everyone showed concern, especially one woman who thinks God's greatest creation— after human beings—is cats. We all prayed.

The next night, at home, I heard mewing and scratching at our door, and when I opened it, there was Frodo. I rejoiced and immediately called Jeanette in Texas to tell her the good news. The next Wednesday I happily reported back to the group.

Don't you think it's possible that we see so many answers to prayers about little, everyday events that we almost start to take them for granted? We forget that God has been faithful and gracious in hearing and answering. I know I'm sometimes guilty of that. Just six months after finding Frodo, I'd already forgotten God's answer. As we shared requests one night at prayer meeting, I mentioned that we weren't seeing answers to prayer about some pressing needs. I wondered if something had gone wrong or if we needed to pray more fervently. The group pondered that until someone steered us in another direction, listing the many requests we had seen answered in recent days, including those I mentioned above. One woman said, "And Mark, there's the case of your cat."

Only as she started retelling the story did I even recall the incident. "Guess I'm out of line," I finally admitted. "God has answered a lot."

That reinforced to me the importance of making prayer lists—and showed me the value of keeping them after the prayers have been answered. When we go back and look at a prayer list from weeks, months, or even years ago, we get perspective on just how many times and how miraculously God has answered our prayers. It's like a history lesson, a pep rally, and a reminder all rolled into one.

How many prayers of yours has God answered? Probably way more than you even remember praying. No matter how long your list, no matter how difficult or mundane your requests, rejoice: God hears them all—and answers.

CHAPTER EIGHT

THE DOWNTIME PRINCIPLE

Tom seized many little opportunities throughout the day to talk to God. These were the moments he didn't really have something to do—downtime—when he was taking a break, driving, or waiting for something. His most frequent downtime came while waiting in line: at the post office, at the supermarket, or in the lunch line at work. Times when apparently all he could do was stand and wait. But actually he could do something truly important during those times: pray. At the doctor's office, in traffic, or waiting for his turn to use the copier, Tom chose to pray rather than allowing himself to get frustrated or angry at the delays.

When Tom took his place in the cafeteria

line, he launched immediately into one of his downtime prayers. He prayed for people in front of him and behind him. "Lord, work in the hearts of all these people who don't know you. That man there with the blond hair; that woman with the ponytail; that heavyset man with the mustache . . . I don't know what departments they work in, but please work in their lives."

As he moved along in the line, Tom prayed for the attendants and cooks in the kitchen, the woman at the cash register, and the folks he saw sitting down in the lunchroom. It wasn't taxing. Sometimes Tom thought of it merely as a creative way to pass the time. But mostly he thought of prayer as a great way to make the most of those little moments that might otherwise be lost daydreaming, doing nothing, or getting annoyed with waiting.

Later that afternoon Tom phoned an important customer and spent a few minutes on hold. It was another piece of downtime—prayer time—and he prayed for the customer while he waited. He prayed for the man's family and about his life based on what Tom knew.

He often prayed for repeat customers while on hold,

and when they shared something personal, he always promised them he'd talk to God about it. This usually elicited one of two responses: abject silence or fervent thanks, sometimes followed by an impromptu discussion about faith. When a person responded with silence, Tom would say, "I don't mean to offend you, but I believe prayer has real power."

Often people then replied, "I'm not offended. I've just never had anyone pray for me like this."

Tom prayed at least once about each need a customer or any other person he encountered had voiced. One time a customer broke into tears when Tom offered to pray for her runaway son. Moved, Tom promised, "I'll keep praying. Would you call me when something changes?" After he prayed with the woman over the phone, she tearfully thanked him for his concern. Later that week she called to say they'd found her son. She added, "Nobody outside my own family ever acted like they cared as much as you did. I'll always remember that." Over the next few months, Tom had the opportunity to talk more with her about his faith.

On his way home from work, as Tom sat in rush-hour

traffic, he resumed his task of being a ten-second prayer warrior. He prayed about the people he could see from his car—the man talking on his cell phone, the woman with a dog in her front seat, and the young woman with glasses and brown hair. It didn't matter to Tom that he didn't know their names or their specific needs. He left that to God. He knew he might be the only person praying for some of these people.

Finally, in the Hy-Vee supermarket where Tom had stopped on the way home, as he walked the aisles pushing a shopping cart, he prayed for people he passed. "That woman looking at the soup, please bless her, Lord." Sometimes he laughed at the way he described these people. "The woman with the screaming child—give her patience and a willingness to teach her child not to be rude."

"That man with the gut, that one right there—please bless him the way you see best. And don't let him have a heart attack because of his weight. Help him to get back into shape."

Tom liked to think that maybe some stranger he passed on the street would be praying for him someday when he needed it. And who knew how many of those prayers by and for strangers might change the world—at least for someone.

Downtime is great time for praying. After all, didn't Paul tell us in Ephesians 5:15–16 to make the most of our time? Is there any better way to use those moments than to pray?

Think of the many times during the day that you have downtime:

- standing in line,

- waiting in a doctor's office or for some other appointment,

- driving and sitting in traffic,

- waiting to be served at a restaurant,

- cleaning up after dinner,

- eating lunch and other meals,

- mowing the lawn or working in the garden,

- staring into space and thinking about things,

- listening to music,

- trying to fall asleep,

- taking a bath or shower,

- sitting at the computer,

- watching your kids play,

- taking a walk, or

- watching television.

All of these moments are ripe for prayer. You don't have to use every second of such downtimes to pray. Just pray as it occurs to you to do so. Pray for the people and things you see around you. I've prayed for dogs, cats, and even hamsters. I've prayed for multitudes of people I'll probably never see again during my whole sojourn on this earth. I've prayed about needs mentioned in church and elsewhere and then forgotten about them the next moment.

But God doesn't forget.

Let me give you two recent examples of brief prayers I offered in my downtimes with barely a second thought—until I saw how God had answered them.

Over the last couple of years, our house has become cluttered with a lot of junk. It needed a major cleaning. My wife and I, working feverishly every day as self-employed freelance writers, just didn't have time to keep up with the housecleaning. During several downtime prayer sessions, it seemed God was whispering to me the idea of doing something special about the problem. I prayed about it several times and seemed especially to think of it when I was driving or sitting in the doctor's office, two primary downtimes I use for praying. As I prayed, I got the idea to surprise Jeanette for Mother's Day with a clean house.

We happened to be traveling to Colorado for a writers' conference around that time, so I hired someone to do the job while we were away. My plan seemed great. The woman I hired was a close friend of Jeanette's and had long wanted to do something special for her, so she was excited about helping.

When I delivered our front-door key to the woman's house, I explained something extremely important: our door had two deadbolts. The lower one was broken. It could be locked from the outside, but it could not opened from the inside. So if it got locked while we were in the house, we couldn't get out unless someone went around to the front door and opened it from the outside. I made clear that only the top deadbolt key would work. I didn't even think about giving her the other key, because I didn't intend to use the lower lock.

When I left the woman's house, I prayed during my downtime driving home. I rattled off several things pertaining to our upcoming trip, and then I said, "Lord, I pray that everything will go smoothly with this cleaning. Help it to go off without a hitch." Figuring everything was covered, I didn't think much about it after that.

On the day of the trip, my sixteen-year-old daughter, Alisha, was the last one out the door, so she was the one to lock it. While I waited in the minivan for everyone to finish up and get in, I prayed a typical traveling prayer: that God would give us a good trip, that he'd keep us safe and keep the van in good working order, that he'd protect the house while we were gone—oh yes, and that God would help things to go well for the cleaning woman and that Jeanette would be delighted and blessed by her surprise when we returned home.

Alisha climbed into the van, and I started the engine and prepared to back down the driveway. Jeanette asked, "Gardner, did you get your charger for the Game Boy?" Gardner plays that thing constantly, and without it he would have had a very sorry vacation.

"No, I don't need it," Gardner said. "It's all charged."

"We'll be gone for six days, honey. It won't stay charged that long. You'd better go in and get it."

I thought it was pretty miraculous that Jeanette had thought of such a thing. I didn't realize that it was a direct answer to my prayer just moments earlier.

Gardner followed me to the front door. When I tried to unlock it, I discovered that Alisha had locked both locks. If we hadn't returned for the charger, I wouldn't have been able to unlock the lower deadbolt, and our friend would not have been able to get into the house to clean. My surprise would have been foiled, and all my good intentions, plans, and efforts would have been for nothing.

Walking into the house, I breathed a prayer of relief. "Thanks, Lord. As usual, you've thought of everything and made sure we didn't make a big mistake."

It thrilled me to realize that not only is God concerned about me and my family, but he also cares about little things like Game Boy chargers, locks, surprises, and clean houses.

Is that experience unusual? No, I believe God does such things all the time in my life. In fact, on that same trip, he did it again.

During that week we were in Colorado, Jeanette went to use the van, and it wouldn't start. She came back into our hotel room and asked me to take a look at it.

I went out and tried the ignition. The engine turned over fine, but it wouldn't catch. I opened the hood, peered in, and pretended to know what I was doing. Seeing nothing out of place—as if I would know—I let the van sit for about an hour.

When I came out later to try again, it started right up.

I prayed as I got out, "Please, Lord, help us not to have any more problems like this, especially on the drive home." The van started fine every time we used it thereafter, and I didn't think any more about my prayer.

After returning home the following Sunday, I tooled around town running errands over the next few days without any problems. Then on Wednesday afternoon the van refused to start. I turned the engine over and over, but it merely cranked. It wouldn't catch. It was exactly what had happened in Colorado.

I waited several hours and tried again. Nothing.

I let it sit overnight and cranked it the next day. Still nothing.

I had to have it towed to the local garage, where my mechanic checked it over and then asked me, "Has your gas gauge been working properly lately?"

"No," I confessed. "Actually, it doesn't work at all. I have to set the mileage and fill my tank with gas based on my calculations rather than by the gauge readings. I didn't want to replace the gauge, because I thought it would cost a lot."

"Well, that's it, then," he said. "Your fuel pump is

going out. It also regulates your gas gauge. How long has this been going on?"

"More than a year."

"Wow!" he said. "Your fuel pump has been on the verge of going out all that time. You were lucky you were here in town. You could have been anywhere when it went."

I told him to go ahead and fix it, and then I remembered my prayer. That fuel pump could have gone out anywhere. On the trip it would have been a real nuisance, since we left the conference on a Sunday. We could have been stranded and forced to wait for a weekday to get the car fixed, possibly at higher cost than normal. But God gave us the help we needed, got us home, and kept the pump working until a more convenient—and safe—time.

That's not to say that Christians don't have car trouble far from home. Of course they do. I've had problems at other times myself. But I believe God heard that brief, one-shot prayer while on vacation in the Rockies, and he answered by helping us to get home safely before the pump collapsed.

Downtime is an ideal time to pray. Why? Because it's

often in those situations, when we're simply sitting and staring into space, that God brings to our minds important concerns. So make the most of that downtime. Let God speak. Listen. Respond. And see how your prayers impact the everyday needs you see around you.

CHAPTER NINE

THE WHATEVER-COMES-AT-YOU PRINCIPLE

I t was a good thing Tom had been praying in his downtime on the way to work that morning. When he stepped into the office, everything seemed to hit him at once. Sam pulled him aside and told him he'd heard from a reliable source that job cuts were inevitable now and probably would come sooner rather than later. Sam was sure their section would be among the first to go. Tom could tell that his colleague was freaked out about it, so he prayed silently and immediately, even as Sam was speaking: *Lord, give us comfort and peace about this situation. Work things out for our good and your glory,*

and help those who do lose their jobs find the right posi-
tions quickly.

He had barely had time to turn on his computer and process what Sam had said when he got a call from an irate customer—a repeat problem customer. Tom knew what he was in for. So as the man bellowed over the phone about the lousy service Tom's company had given him, peppering his rant with insults and curses well beyond the professional realm, Tom felt his anger rising. *God, help me to keep my temper in check and to give a gentle answer in spite of this guy's verbal attack,* he prayed urgently.

Tom found himself speaking to the customer with a kind of sure-footed diplomacy he didn't normally possess. He could feel the fury draining from the man on the other end of the line until he seemed almost polite—even grateful. It was a vast improvement. Tom promised he'd send the materials the customer needed overnight, then breathed a quick prayer for the man and whatever was troubling him. He also thanked God for his help.

At midmorning, when his wife called to tell him she'd sprained her ankle and was going to the doctor, Tom prayed right then over the phone: "Lord, I pray that this is just a sprain and that Darla will get over it quickly. But if it's more serious than that, help the doctors get to the bottom of things right away." He offered to leave work and take her to the doctor, but she told him to stay. "It's no problem," she assured him. "I can get to the car and drive myself. I just knew you'd want to know and be praying."

Tom was pleased that his wife included him in anything that needed prayer. In his mind, that encompassed just about everything.

Darla called back later with the doctor's report. "It's just a sprain," she said. "I should be fine in a week."

"Great to hear, honey. Thanks for letting me know." *Thank you, God,* Tom acknowledged gratefully in his mind.

That afternoon Darla called again, this time to ask Tom to talk with their son, Brad. He'd been playing with a neighbor boy, and the two had gotten into a fight. She had checked his bruises and dried his tears, but she hoped Tom would be able to offer some fatherly insight and encouragement about the anger and hurt Brad was nursing inside.

"What happened?" Tom tried to let Brad hear his concern.

"We were just playing," Brad said defensively. "Then Tony got really mad, threw the ball at me really hard, and hit me in the shin. It hurts a lot, Dad."

Lord, give me wisdom to deal with this situation in a way that helps Brad grow to be more like you, Tom prayed silently. "Let's pray for Tony," he said aloud.

"Why?" Brad sounded unwilling.

"Sounds like he needs God's help to get his temper under control a little better."

Tom prayed, "Father, please help Tony to learn to be kind and not to get so mad when things don't go his way. And please help Brad to forgive him and be a good example."

"No way," Brad said. "I'm not forgiving him, Dad."

"Why not?"

"He doesn't deserve it—he hurt me on purpose. And he's not sorry."

"How many of your sins did God forgive?" Tom asked.

Brad hesitated, then softly admitted, "All of them."

"And how many have there been?"

Brad sighed. "Thousands."

"Don't you think that if God forgave you thousands of sins, you should forgive Tony this one?"

Brad was silent for a while. "I guess."

"Good. Now go out there and tell him you forgive him."

"What?!"

"Go out and tell him."

"It'll just make him madder!"

Tom laughed. "You're not responsible for what he does with what you tell him, Brad. You're only responsible for your part."

"Okay. Bye." Brad put down the phone without hanging up, and Tom could hear him walk away.

Around four o'clock Tom was called to his boss's office. His heart fluttered a little. He had a pretty good idea this wasn't going to be good news. "Lord, help me to be calm," he prayed. "May I be a source of strength for others at this time and a good witness for you."

The look on his boss's face confirmed Tom's fears. "I'm sorry Tom," Gina said, genuinely distressed for him.

"The bottom line on the company isn't good. You know that. The CEO has told us that drastic cuts are necessary. You're a great worker, and I tried hard to argue for you to be moved to another department, but it did no good." She took a deep breath. "As of today, you're terminated."

Tom held out his hand. "Thanks for the compliment, Gina. Can I count on you for a solid reference?"

"Absolutely."

"Thanks for fighting for me. Not many bosses would have done that. He shook Gina's hand and headed back to his office for the last time. Tom was amazed at how calm and peaceful he felt. He knew there was only one explanation: God. With God's help, he could handle whatever came at him on any given day.

Even a day like today.

Life is expert at throwing things at us that we're ill equipped or unprepared to handle. The good news is that God is an expert at handling anything life can dish out. All we have to do is turn to him in prayer. It can (and should) be as natural as breathing. Just as we don't have to think about crying out when something hurts us physically, so prayer can become our first response when anything overwhelms us spiritually or emotionally. That's one of the best aspects of ten-second praying. It doesn't keep the difficulties from coming at us, but it sure feels good to share those heavy burdens with a heavenly father who's stronger and wiser than we are.

We recently took in a dog that Angela, a woman in our church, could no longer handle. Zoe-Girl, named after the Christian band ZOEgirl, was extremely rambunctious. Angela hadn't been able to get Zoe-Girl (the dog, not the band) to stop jumping up on people—which was a problem, since the black Lab weighs eighty pounds. When I picked her up at the veterinary clinic recently after kenneling her there for a few days, a kid in the waiting room said, "Wow! Mom, look at that giant dog!"

Zoe-Girl *is* a giant. Jumping affectionately on people—especially little kids or anyone unsteady on his or her feet—can be devastating. It was imperative that we break her of that habit.

I began praying about it, not really knowing what to

do. But Jeanette found a local animal shelter that gave free lessons on training exuberant, seemingly uncontrollable dogs. My son, daughter, and I took the lessons and learned how to control Zoe-Girl better. The instructor warned us never to give Zoe any attention, treats, or food unless she was sitting calmly and under control.

Over the next few weeks, we all fed Zoe by hand— and only when she was well behaved and calm. When she wanted to be petted, we didn't pet her until she sat. When she jumped up on us, we turned around and told her to sit. Until she obeyed, we gave her no attention.

I also kept praying, and soon Zoe was much better. In fact, when she greeted us at the door after we'd been gone, she slid automatically into sitting position. We still have to work with her, but she's improving consistently. I often wonder how she would be if we hadn't prayed about her behavior and training.

The point of this story isn't that we should turn to God if we need to train our dogs. The point is that we should turn to God no matter what situation we're facing in life. He's there for us. He wants to walk with us on this journey, helping us face whatever we encounter today—

and every day. Life is full of uncontrollable Zoes that jump on us when we least expect them, threatening to knock us down or keep us off balance. None of us gets to opt out of the scratching, the hair, and the slobber that life too often sends our way. Our only choice is whether we confront life's challenges alone or with the help of our loving heavenly Father.

Sure, you can break a dog of its habit of jumping without praying about it, but I'd rather do it with God's help than without. When I pray about the challenges I face, God changes things—the situation, my attitude, me. He teaches me something, even if it's only patience. Praying about everything life throws our way lifts life from the mundane to a spiritual plane. It's a much nicer place to walk: I highly recommend the view to anyone who seeks real adventure in life instead of just plodding along trying to survive the day.

CHAPTER TEN

THE A-S-K PRINCIPLE

As Tom drove home from work, his back-seat full of personal items from his desk and office, he struggled with feelings of discouragement and fear. A Bible verse, Isaiah 41:10, came to mind: "Do not fear, for I am with you; do not anxiously look about you, for I am your God. I will strengthen you, surely I will help you, surely I will uphold you with My righteous right hand."

The truth of the verse calmed Tom's heart, and he prayed aloud. "Lord, I know you have something out there for me, maybe even something better. Help me find it. Give me some thoughts on what direction I should go."

That night Tom felt the Spirit of God prompting him: "Call Jesse. He could help."

When Tom called his friend, Jesse immediately had a suggestion. "I hear there's an opening over at Springhill for a customer service manager. You might check it out."

Why had God put Jesse into Tom's mind? Because Jesse knew something Tom didn't, and it was a good way to give direction to Tom.

The next day Tom stopped by the company, picked up an application, and filled it out. The person in charge assured him they'd consider him for the position.

A few days later Tom was called in for an interview. He prepared well, finding out all he could about the company—its products, direction, goals, and personnel—before his interview. He also prayed about it and got plenty of sleep the night before.

He was glad he had prepared so thoroughly. The interview seemed to go well, and he felt that he'd made a good impression on the supervisor. However, he learned the following week that they'd hired someone else. Tom had prayed and gone seeking. Why hadn't he been hired? The Spirit prompted him again: "Knock, and it will be opened to you."

Tom had memorized Matthew 7:7–8 early in his

Christian life, and it had become the bedrock of his life. "Ask, and it will be given to you," Jesus said in the Sermon on the Mount. "Seek, and you will find; knock, and it will be opened to you. For everyone who asks receives, and he who seeks finds, and to him who knocks it will be opened."

Tom understood that there were three different aspects of this principle: sometimes he only had to *ask* God for an answer to prayer, and God responded quickly and perfectly. But at other times asking wasn't enough. God wanted him to do something about his prayer, so Tom had to *seek*. In such cases Tom found it necessary to get out and take a look at some situations, talk to people, find out what he could do to help bring about the answer to his prayer.

Occasionally the process took even more. He would have to go *knock* on some doors to get what he needed.

Tom resolved to do some knocking. "Lord, please bless my efforts," he prayed.

He started calling all around town, and soon he had lined up several interviews. In time he was offered a job. It was managerial but not strictly customer service. The new position involved directing a service team in a large retail business. Not only was it more in line with Tom's skills and interests, but the starting salary was just as good as what he'd been paid at his old job—and he'd have more opportunity for raises and promotions!

As Tom settled in at the new job, he realized that once again the process outlined by Jesus had worked. His new job had come not only because he prayed but because he'd gone seeking and knocking as well.

How can you begin using the Ask-Seek-Knock principle in your daily life?

When Jesus told us, "Ask, and it will be given to you," he certainly didn't mean that we should ask for anything and everything our hearts desire—the sky's the limit. God isn't our ATM or "instant win" ticket. I can tell you that with the voice of experience. As a new Christian I believed God wanted me to be a poet and to tell people about Jesus through my poetry. But I needed money to get started. I passed the pharmacy one day and noticed a sign advertising lottery tickets. I'd never bought a lottery ticket in my life, but this time it seemed like a good idea. Couldn't God do anything? Didn't he own the cattle on a thousand hills? Wasn't the king's heart in his hands (Proverbs 21:1)? So why not the lottery too? I purchased the ticket with prayer and great faith.

When I woke up the next morning, I truly believed I had struck the mother lode. But when I read the lottery numbers in the paper, I learned that not only had I not won, but I was as wrong as I could possibly be. I hadn't guessed even a single digit of the jackpot number.

I haven't bought a lottery ticket since. But I learned something that day. We can't ask for just anything. We can't even assume God will answer because we believe our request is good or right or even God's will. And we can't presume to tell God how to answer our prayers. We're just not that smart or wise.

So what was I missing? The Bible calls it asking according to God's will (1 John 5:14). We can ask, but God has to want to do it before he'll give us that yes answer we're seeking. And how can we know God's will? On most of the mundane things in life, perhaps we can't. But one way is sure: pray according to the Scriptures. When we pray according to God's Word, we can't help but be praying according to his will. When I turn a scripture into a prayer, I see answers.

Several years ago I totaled my car. Fortunately, no one was hurt, but my car had become nothing more than a giant paperweight. Useless. It was my fault, but collision insurance is helpful in such situations. I knew my insurance company owed me something.

I checked the book value of my car, and it looked as if the best I could expect was $4,000. I knew I needed more than that to afford a new car, so I turned to a scripture: "My God will supply all your needs according to His riches in glory in Christ Jesus" (Philippians 4:19). Then I prayed: "God, please meet this need."

The insurance company and God answered. They gave me more than $5,000. I was happy and grateful— and, quite frankly, astonished. God had come through!

Granted, God doesn't always answer prayers exactly

the way we think he should—even though we're using Scripture. His will on any issue may be some other alternative that still conforms to his Word. What if God had wanted to teach me to get along on less money? What if that was the need he meant to meet à la Philippians 4:19? Or what if he'd wanted me to find a different car that wouldn't cost as much?

Many times I've prayed through Scripture, and God answered in ways I didn't expect. So when you do this, remember that God is still God. As C. S. Lewis writes in each volume of his Chronicles of Narnia, "He's not a tame lion." You can't put him in a box. But if his will is the defining issue, then Scripture will show you clearly what that will is, even if the details of answer don't conform to your preconceived ideas about it.

Now let's look at the second part of the A-S-K Principle that we saw Tom follow in the story above: Seek. Sometimes God wants us to do more before he answers our prayers: We must take action.

If we ask God to help us get into shape, we must seek the answer to our prayer by jogging, working out, or playing a sport. We can't simply pray and expect God to magically whisk away that spare tire around our waist.

After going through a bitter divorce, I was a single father for several years. I had custody of my two little girls. One weekend, when Nicole was ten and Alisha five, we drove north to New Jersey to visit my brother and his family at their home by the lake. His two girls are similar in age to my two girls, so it was a lovely weekend as the foursome splashed and played every waking hour.

We planned to stay from Friday to Tuesday. I had work to do at home, and I needed to get back. When Tuesday arrived, I told Nicole and Alisha that we had to get ready to leave, but they wanted to stay. As I pressed the troops into service packing so we could hit the road, the four girls petitioned me in a back room. "Daddy," my daughters pleaded, "please can we stay until Friday?"

I told them it wasn't my decision, but I was overwhelmed by their determination and how much they all wanted this. I really wanted to be able to give them something they obviously wanted so much, so I prayed: "God, please work this out somehow."

We all tromped in to see Diane, my brother's wife. The girls made their case. They solemnly vowed perfect obedience for the whole time they were together if we would only grant their request. I prayed as Diane considered. She studied a calendar thoughtfully. "Look, we're coming down to Mom's the weekend after this one. Why don't they just stay for the whole week and a half, and we'll bring them home then?"

The girls whooped in sheer joy. I smiled in silent adoration of my Master, and everything was hunky-dory.

It's not a perfect illustration, but it does demonstrate the principle. Sometimes we must do more than just ask; we must seek. We can't just wait for God's answer to drop out of the sky. If we want healing, we must seek out a competent doctor. If we want a raise at work, we must seek out the boss and talk about it.

But as we saw in Tom's example, there's a third part of the A-S-K principle: Knock. "Knock, and it will be opened to you."

Asking isn't enough. Seeking isn't enough. Sometimes we have to get tough. Play hardball. We must knock . . . and hard!

For some time I prayed for a young man in my church youth group. He was smart, handsome, and an all-around good kid. But he was skeptical about Christianity. I prayed every day for his salvation, but nothing happened.

Then I sought him out, talked with him, visited him, and watched him compete in a debate at school because it was something he loved dearly. It was important to him, so I made it important to me.

One day I went to his home and had dinner with his family. Afterward we talked. I asked him explicitly about his relationship with the Lord. He told me he just wasn't sure. Over the next few weeks I made a special effort to get to know him. I knocked repeatedly on his spiritual door.

One day in Sunday school he came up to me, smiling, and said he'd finally put his faith in Christ. I asked him what had changed his mind. He answered, "You! I never had anyone come to me and talk like that."

Another prayer that leads to much knocking is a kind I'm always praying as a Christian writer. I've never reached a point in my writing ministry where publishers seek me out to ask, "What are you writing lately? Whatever it is, we'd like to publish it."

That probably happens to people like Max Lucado and Chuck Swindoll all the time. But for guys like me, it takes constant praying, seeking, and knocking to get a book published.

A ready example is this very book. I got this idea a few years ago and thought it really a cool, snappy, easy-to-grasp-and-use kind of principle. I saw it as a *Prayer of Jabez* kind of book. I wrote a proposal and sent it to several publishers, including the one that published *The Prayer of Jabez,* the book about prayer that became a phenomenon and sold more than ten million copies in about two years. That publisher— and many others—rejected my proposal.

I reworked it and sent it out again. This time two publishers liked it and took it to their publishing boards. I was pumped.

Alas, the letters and e-mails soon arrived informing me that although their boards liked the idea, they had to pass. One commented that there were just too many prayer books on the market at the time.

I went back to the drawing board and tried to deal with that concern in a new proposal. Once more a publisher liked it and took it to their board. And once again it wasn't picked up.

Beginning to think this was an exercise in futility, I prayed, "God, do you want me to keep trying, or should I just give up on this one?"

God seemed to say, "Keep knocking. I'm behind this."

I sent the proposal out one more time. I waited. It was now nearly two years after my original mailings. Then Denny Boultinghouse of Howard Books expressed interest. After another three or four months, I got an e-mail from Denny. Not only was he interested in this book, but he also wanted to publish another I'd sent him. I soon had a contract for two books!

If you're like me, such waiting drives me crazy. I want God to answer *now*. But I keep being reminded that sometimes I only have to ask and it's done; more often I must seek. But many times it takes some hard knocking. That's just the way God does things, I've learned.

Of course, God doesn't answer all our prayers the way we might like or expect him to, no matter how much faith we have or how convinced we are that what we're asking is God's will. But if we put legs on our prayers—if we ask, seek, and knock—we will see God working! It's his promise. That's what Tom found out as he prayed his ask-seek-and-knock prayers. It's what you'll discover too.

CHAPTER ELEVEN

PRAYING THE SCRIPTURES

One of the biggest bugaboos for people who pray much and take prayer seriously is determining God's will. What does God want? What is his will on the subject?

We know that if we don't pray "according to God's will," the prayer won't be answered positively. Like John says in 1 John 5:14–15, "This is the confidence which we have before Him, that, if we ask anything according to His will, He hears us. And if we know that He hears us in whatever we ask, we know that we have the requests which we have asked from Him."

I've known this verse well and for a long time, and it often puzzled me. How could I know if something was God's will until I'd asked for it and God had answered? Only when the whole process concluded could I ever be sure.

One day, though, I realized how I could pray "according to God's will" every time: by praying on the basis of God's Word. The Bible, when it gives a command or tells us what God wants for our lives, is God's will through and through. Everything in it reflects God's will, except certain places like stories or dialogue that relate to someone else, not God—like the diatribes of Job's counselors against him, or the devil's lies when he tempted Jesus (see Matthew 4:1–11).

So if I could line up anything and everything I prayed with a truth in the Bible, I could be sure I was praying according to God's will. Sometimes finding a passage that spoke to the problem was difficult. Occasionally even impossible. But many times I knew precisely where to look or what to cite when I prayed, because I also spent time reading my Bible and memorizing important verses.

That's why this chapter is so crucial. Praying according to the Scriptures is one of the best ways to talk to God, since his Word without question shows his will for us. Sure, the Bible doesn't give us much to go on when we want to pray that the baby will get through toilet training soon. But when we pray that the baby will "grow in the grace and knowledge of our Lord and Savior Jesus Christ" (2 Peter 3:18), we can be sure that's in line with God's plan.

How do you begin to become a Christian who can relate your prayers to precise scriptures? By gaining a ready and growing knowledge of the Bible. How do you do that? You can start by reading the Bible, meditating on and memorizing the passages that speak most forcefully to you.

I often shrink from telling people the "same old stuff" about Christian living, but it really isn't that complicated, and there are few secrets. Walking with Jesus is a matter of discipline and attention: studying the Bible, reading it regularly, learning by heart certain passages that stand out to you, and meditating on them in quiet moments when you can think clearly. It's not a matter of doing a set number of exercises, like you would jumping jacks or stomach crunches. It's just plain old regular attention to the Word of God.

When you do this, you give the Holy Spirit some

starting material so he can work in your mind. When you know a verse or truth, he can remind you of it when needed. But if you don't know it, you can't be reminded of it.

I have found a number of scriptures that are good to include in any memorization program. These will give you a good start:

- "I am confident of this very thing, that He who began a good work in you will perfect it until the day of Christ Jesus" (Philippians 1:6).

- "God causes all things to work together for good to those who love God, to those who are called according to His purpose" (Romans 8:28).

- "By grace you have been saved through faith; and that not of yourselves, it is the gift of God; not as a result of works, so that no one may boast" (Ephesians 2:8–9).

- "'I know the plans that I have for you,' declares the LORD, 'plans for welfare and not for calamity to give you a future and a hope'" (Jeremiah 29:11).

■ "Call to Me and I will answer you, and I will tell you great and mighty things, which you do not know" (Jeremiah 33:3).

■ "The LORD is my shepherd, I shall not want" (Psalm 23:1).

■ "Do not fear, for I am with you; do not anxiously look about you, for I am your God. I will strengthen you, surely I will help you, surely I will uphold you with My righteous right hand" (Isaiah 41:10).

■ "I am with you always, even to the end of the age" (Matthew 28:20).

■ "I am not ashamed of the gospel, for it is the power of God for salvation to everyone who believes, to the Jew first and also to the Greek. For in it the righteousness of God is revealed from faith to faith; as it is written, 'But the righteous man shall live by faith'" (Romans 1:16–17).

■ "Be anxious for nothing, but in everything by prayer and supplication with thanksgiving let your requests be made known to God. And the peace of God, which surpasses all comprehension, will guard your hearts and your minds in Christ Jesus" (Philippians 4:6–7).

■ "God has not given us a spirit of timidity, but of power and love and discipline" (2 Timothy 1:7).

Begin with these and use them where appropriate as you pray. Add to the list as you grow in grace. The Spirit of God will fill your mind with every good thing as you practice these disciplines.

As an example, years ago I went through a severe clinical depression, during which I became suicidal. I was in despair, feeling that God had left me permanently. Only those who have experienced this know the depth of darkness one can plunge into, and I was in deep. I felt for a long time (it took two and half years to recover) that I was literally in hell and that the terrors of hell were all around me every day. I suffered from feelings of isolation and inner blackness, thinking nothing could help me—an overwhelming sense that God had abandoned me.

In time I began using various scriptures to pray and ask God, on the basis of his promises as recorded in the Bible, to fulfill those promises in my life. One passage was particularly meaningful: Philippians 4:6–7, verses many Christians store in their memories to be recalled in tough times. It's about not worrying but instead praying about everything so that God's peace will guard our minds and hearts. I've included the full text in the list above.

Many times, following the exact "formula" in that passage, I fought off the anxiety in my soul, then asked God to set me free from the dark hold the depression had on me. Incorporating words of thanksgiving, I pled over and over that the peace "which surpasses all comprehension" would come into my heart.

I prayed this for a long time before the depression fully lifted; but even in the midst of it, I did receive some respite from the anguish, enjoying periods of normalcy and less depression than usual. Still, I felt battered daily by the idea that God had left me, and I feared I'd lost my salvation. I read passages about salvation over and over and prayed them, too, as I asked God to make sure I was his.

In the autumn of 1977, two years after the depression hit, I knelt by my bed and prayed, "God, I don't know why this continues. I don't know where I'm going. I don't know what you have planned. But I submit to you, even if your plan is for me to be depressed for the rest of my life. I only ask that you give me the strength and grace to endure."

I sensed that I'd reached a turning point, and I relaxed at my bedside, wrung out and hoping only to survive the rest of the day. But I was serious. I meant what I said. It became the greatest act of submission I'd ever made before God.

Three months later the depression lifted—not all at once, but gradually. By the time I took my new job as a youth pastor in Indiana, it was gone. I have never experienced it again at that level.

I don't know that my prayers during that time were any more effective than at other times, but I do know that my fervency and application of Scripture in those prayers had seemed a powerful spiritual weapon. Lamentations 3:22–23 tells us that God's "compassions never fail. They are new every morning; great is Your faithfulness." I depended on verses like that to get me through hours and days of darkness. It seemed that as I turned the Bible's words into requests and petitions that spiritual power went both out from me and into me. Although I wasn't released from my trial immediately, the mountain of prayers I brought to the throne of God eventually had their effect, and I was freed. I believe now that the trial I went through made me a stronger, more resilient and obedient believer than I'd ever been before.

That experience taught me to plead the Word when I pray. It is the sure will of God, and we can make no mistake that it is what he wants for our lives. When we talk to God on the basis of what he's already promised or commanded, I think he is more apt to answer than when we just fire a shot in the dark.

Memorizing passages of Scripture is immensely helpful. But our prayers don't have to be limited to the verses we can quote. We pray through Scripture simply by reading a passage and turning it into prayer. A number of the apostle

Paul's prayers are excellent passages to use when interceding for people. (A few of these include Ephesians 1:15–19; 3:16–19; Philippians 1:9–11; and 1 Thessalonians 1:2–3; 3:10–13. Many others can be found in the New Testament epistles as well.) One passage I like to use is Paul's prayer in Colossians 1:9–12. Consider these powerful words: "We have not ceased to pray for you and to ask that you may be filled with the knowledge of His will in all spiritual wisdom and understanding, so that you will walk in a manner worthy of the Lord, to please Him in all respects, bearing fruit in every good work and increasing in the knowledge of God; strengthened with all power, according to His glorious might, for the attaining of all steadfastness and patience; joyously giving thanks to the Father, who has qualified us to share in the inheritance of the saints in Light."

This is a tremendous passage to pray for anyone. Paul originally wrote it to the Colossians, and I'm sure he prayed this way for many others; and you can use it as a template for prayers for your family, yourself, and anyone else. Imagine if God answered all those things on behalf of someone you love. Imagine if he did it for you!

Now, don't just imagine it—pray it. If you offer this

prayer for any Christian, God will surely answer positively, because it is his will for all of us, including that person. That doesn't mean he'll do it all in one day, but over time God will embed these truths and realities in the lives of those for whom you pray.

Ephesians 1:15–19 tells us more about Paul's prayers: "For this reason I too, having heard of the faith in the Lord Jesus which exists among you and your love for all the saints, do not cease giving thanks for you, while making mention of you in my prayers, that the God of our Lord Jesus Christ, the Father of glory, may give to you a spirit of wisdom and of revelation in the knowledge of Him. I pray that the eyes of your heart may be enlightened, so that you will know what is the hope of His calling, what are the riches of the glory of the His inheritance in the saints, and what is the surpassing greatness of His power toward us who believe."

Let's examine the specific things Paul prayed for the Ephesians:

- that God would give them a spirit of wisdom and of revelation in the knowledge of God, and

- that the eyes of their hearts would be enlightened.

Why did he pray this way? So that they would know

- the hope of God's calling,

- the "riches of the glory of the His inheritance in the saints,"

- and the greatness of God's power toward those who believe.

Doesn't this cover the multitude of needs and concerns in the body of Christ? What if we began praying for these realities in the lives of every believer—and even for unbelievers—that their hearts would be enlightened? We probably can't even imagine all that might happen when God answered such prayers, but we know it would include the "hope of His calling" (heaven, perfection, eternal life, sinlessness, righteousness, true love and joy); the "riches of the glory of His inheritance" (all that Christ has prepared for us in heaven and also in the blessings of daily living); and the "surpassing greatness of His power" (the strength and ability to overcome sin and temptation, the power to live a holy, God-pleasing life, the joy of pleasing him in every respect).

What a tremendous prayer! Yet it's just one of many in the Bible that we can use for God's glory in the world as we pray.

I find that these kinds of prayers have intrinsic power, both for me as a ten-second prayer warrior and for the objects of my prayer. Don't you think it would be amazing if every Christian began taking prayer seriously and offered petitions like this for all those they know? I think it could radically change the world.

What are some good passages to use as templates for such prayers? Here are ten places to start:

- Matthew 6:9–13. This is what we call "The Lord's Prayer." I don't believe it's a prayer we should just repeat over and over, but it's a template to use in addressing God. What I mean is, when we say, "Our Father who is in heaven," we might add, "for I know you reign supreme,

Lord, and that you are over all; and I trust that you will bring to a great conclusion all the plans you have for your kingdom." When we say, "Hallowed be Your name," we could say something like, "Your name is holy to me, Lord. You are the mighty one, high and lifted up, and I bow down and worship you." (Of course, use your own words.) And so on. Use this and all other scriptures as guides or jumping-off points for prayer.

- Psalm 8. This is a good prayer when you want to worship God.

- Psalm 23, a great guide for praying for God's protection and giving thanks for his love for us.

- Romans 12:1–2. Use this passage to pray about your commitment and dedication to God.

- Romans 12:9–21 offers a fantastic litany of ways to pray about your conduct toward fellow Christians.

■ Ephesians 4:15–32. This is a great passage to use in praying about your conduct (and that of others) in the world.

■ Ephesians 5:22–33 is a good passage to use when praying about your marriage and how you and your spouse treat each other.

■ James 1:12–27 contains a series of great things to pray for yourself and others.

■ 1 John 1:5–10. Good things to pray about for others about walking in the light.

■ John 17 records Jesus's final prayer while on earth, a great example when praying for the world and for the church.

Again, these are only starting places. Oh, and don't forget the Prayer of Jabez (1 Chronicles 4:10). It's a short prayer, but a fine one to use every now and then in your prayer life. In fact, for a while after I read Bruce Wilkinson's book about Jabez's little petition, I prayed regularly that God would bless me, enlarge my border, have his hand on me, and keep me from evil. I wasn't convinced this prayer was a biblical mandate, but it still seemed like a solid guide for personal prayer and one worth using now and then.

Shortly after I began using this prayer as a guide, I took a class in public speaking with Carol Kent, a well-known instructor and speaker. While working through several of our practice sessions in which we each gave short speeches to our group of seven or eight for evaluation, one woman approached me and said, "I believe the Lord is going to give you many great opportunities in the near future to speak. He has told me you will soon be speaking before crowds."

I didn't think much about it, but shortly thereafter, I attended a large writers' conference where the director found herself without a keynote speaker due to the originally scheduled person's illness. She asked me to speak. I had a rare opportunity to talk to about four hundred people that day—not the largest crowd I'd ever addressed, but certainly a good venue. And people who heard me at that gathering asked me to speak at their conferences in other places in the country.

I'm still not sure how much we should use the prayer of Jabez as a template in our prayer life, but I do know that after one particular period when I prayed it, God brought great blessings into my life. I believe he responds faithfully to every prayer we offer according to his Word.

CHAPTER TWELVE

MEMORIZING
THE SCRIPTURES

I believe the key to successful prayer of any kind is knowing the Bible. Over the years I've used several methods to get the Word of God into my heart. When we know the Scriptures well, our prayers naturally flow in the direction of Bible-based intercession. We begin wanting to link every prayer to some mandate in Scripture. That way we can be confident we're praying according to God's will—praying prayers he will assuredly answer, even if not necessarily in our preferred time frame.

Scripture memorization has strengthened my prayer life, and it will do the same for yours. That's good news. But here's more good news: memorizing portions of God's Word doesn't have to be difficult. The methods I use are easy and even fun. Let me share them with you.

The Bible Memory Pack

I remember when I first began memorizing Scripture. I became a Christian in the summer of 1972, after my graduation from college. That fall I decided not to blitz the business world with my talents. Instead, I became a ski bum at Stratton Mountain in Stratton, Vermont. I was a short-order cook at breakfast, lunch, and dinner and a maniacal sidewinding skier the rest of the time. I loved it.

One day I received some information from a Christian campus organization, including a brochure listing books and tools for discipleship and witnessing. I decided to purchase a few. I combed through the list and came to a nondescript offering in the back called a Bible Memory Pack. The blurb explained the secret and necessity of Bible memorization. So I added this item to my lengthy order.

Three weeks later I received several books, over a hundred tracts, and a Bible Memory Pack. I tore open the tracts and got ready for the slopes. I put the books on my shelf, planning to read them at my earliest opportunity. But I gave the Bible Memory Pack a mere glance, then tucked it into my dresser drawer. *No need for this at the moment,* I thought. I headed off for some ski wizardry.

I handed tracts to people I went up the lifts with. I was happy, whistling. But that evening, something went wrong. My mind drifted to lustful thoughts, swearing, and all sorts of evil ideas. I prayed for God's help in the midst of the barrage, but it seemed he had suddenly gone deaf. Nothing I did stopped the mental assault. I couldn't understand it. In the five months or so that I'd been a Christian, I had cleaned plenty of garbage out of my life. But now it seemed it was all coming back in a virtual deluge.

The next day I felt depressed. I paced in my room, praying. "Lord, my brainwaves have gone berserk. What on earth is wrong?"

Then a thought sounded clearly in my head. *Remember that Bible Memory Pack you threw in the back of your sock drawer? Maybe you'd better get working on it.*

I swallowed and nodded. I rushed to my dresser, pulled out the pack, and read the instructions. Soon I began working on my first verse: "These things I have written to you who believe in the name of the Son of God, so that you may know that you have eternal life" (1 John 5:13).

Because of my experiences with drugs and alcohol before coming to faith, my mind wasn't the sharp steel trap it should have been, and it took me a week of determined repetition before that verse became firmly etched in my memory. But I was on my way. Using that pack and, later, other devices was to become a focal point of my spiritual life. I'd recommend starting with this essential method for getting the Bible into your heart and then into your prayers.

Many Christians are familiar with this handy tool. It's a small pack of cards, similar to a business-card wallet. Because it's small, you can carry it anywhere. Simply write the verses on the cards, keep them in the pack in your pocket, and pull them out for review whenever you have a moment to spare—while standing in line, while traveling, etc. Just read and repeat the verse on the first card until you can recite it without looking. You can go over the verse in your mind, saying it to yourself. Out loud is better, but you might not want to do that in certain situations. Start with the reference (where the verse is found in the Bible). After you say the verse, repeat the reference again to fix it in your memory and in connection with the text.

When you've mastered the first verse, move on to a second. But remember to review the first one now and then to keep it fixed in your mind.

You'll be surprised how quickly you work up to knowing five or ten verses. Just be sure to keep reviewing all of these regularly, or they'll slip from your memory. But even that is easier than you might think. I've found that I can review thirty or forty verses just while waiting in a doctor's office or at other downtimes. You can even do this while driving, reviewing the verses in your mind or reciting them aloud. (Stick to verses you can remember without having to look at the card.)

If you use this method to memorize two verses per week, you'll have over a hundred verses down pat in a year. If you keep at it, in ten years you'll know more than a thousand verses. Imagine how easily the Spirit can speak to you with all that stored in your mind.

Bible Memory Packs are available in Christian bookstores and from several other organizations, such as Campus Crusade for Christ and the Billy Graham Evangelistic Association. But if you stick with this method, you'll soon run out of verses they give you. And you may prefer to memorize verses in a Bible translation other than what you find in those packs. One easy solution is to write or type verses you like on regular, blank business cards. Most office stores carry perforated sheets you can use with your personal printer and then separate into business cards. Or, if you have an old set of business cards you no longer use, you can write on the backs. As you read the Bible and come across verses you want to remember, simply put them on cards and memorize them.

The key is to stick with it. Lots of people start off memorizing Scripture with gung and ho but end up hung and low. They give up. Why?

Satan will do anything to keep you from living a godly spiritual life. You're in a battle. Expect the devil to throw a fit if you take memorizing Scripture seriously. He'll heave everything he can at you as a distraction— television, the temptation to procrastinate, tiredness, boredom, money problems, you name it. Anything to keep you from getting those verses down in your memory. But remember (and here's a great verse to start with in your memorization plan): "Greater is He who is in you than he who is in the world" (1 John 4:4). If we rely on God, he will see us through.

After you've logged enough verses to fill up the pack, you may want to try the next method so you don't end up lugging a memory pack the size of a suitcase.

The Bible Memory File

Once you've used the Bible memory pack for a lengthy period of time, you'll find that you've gotten so many verses stuffed in there it's like carrying around an extra wallet. More important, it becomes difficult to review all those verses and keep them organized. You don't know when you've reviewed what.

I had reached this point after about a year of memorizing verses I'd selected myself and those from the Campus Crusade for Christ Bible Memory Pack. But then Garry Friesen, a doctoral student on the Dallas Seminary campus, introduced some students to a method he'd learned as a young Christian. I jumped in and learned how to use what he called a Bible Memory File.

I continued using my Bible Memory Pack for learning new verses, because I could carry that with me and use it easily during the day. But the file helped me tremendously in setting up a systematic way of tracking and reviewing every verse I'd ever learned.

Here's how it works. The Bible Memory File is a review system using three-by-five index cards. You divide the main file into three sections, or smaller files: Daily Review, Weekly Review, and Monthly Review. The Daily Review file will contain all the verses you're presently working on and need to review once a day (in conjunction with the Bible Memory Pack). The Weekly Review file gets divided into seven smaller files, one labeled for each day of the week, containing verses you know well enough to review only once a week. You'll review the verses in each of these files only on that day of the week. The Monthly Review file should have thirty numbered sections containing verses you know well enough to review only once a month.

I found that I could review up to sixty verses on any given day in about fifteen to twenty minutes with this file system.

Putting It into Practice

Each day, when you have some time (preferably regularly and consistently, like after breakfast or at lunch), open the Bible Memory File and retrieve the verses for that day. So, let's say it's Monday, March 21. You simply pull out the "Daily," "Monday," and "Day 21" files and review the verses on the cards inside. You might have five new verses in the "Daily" file, twelve in the "Monday" group, and thirty-two for "Day 21." Simply look at the Scripture reference, repeat the verse in your mind (or aloud, if you can) without looking at the card. Then check the card to make sure you got it right.

It's that easy.

This provides a systematic method of reviewing verses on a regular basis. You don't have to worry about where and when you'll be going over each verse, because they're all in your file. Using the Bible Memory File enabled me to keep more than two thousand verses in my head, reviewing them only fifteen minutes a day.

This system is also highly versatile. Not only does it help you keep the verses fresh in your mind because you're consistently reviewing them, but if you find that you've forgotten a verse, you can place it in a higher-frequency file. Occasionally I'd discover that I couldn't recite from memory a verse in my monthly file. So I'd simply transfer it into the daily or weekly file, and I'd have it down again.

Sticking with It

Again, the enemy of your soul will try to throw you off track. Satan will try to take your review time away through distractions or obligations, so you have to guard that time carefully.

For years I got up early and spent the first hour of the day in prayer, Bible study, and Scripture memorization. But I had to fight to keep it that way. That was my practice, though I have tried other methods as well. What's best for you is whatever will work for you. Try various methods, and the Lord will guide you into the one best suited to your schedule and needs.

You'll also have to guard against letting this become a legalistic ritual. That is, if you find yourself thinking, *Uh-oh, I didn't do my verses today. God's going to punish me for that,* you're probably putting too much pressure on yourself. If you miss a day, don't beat yourself up over it. (God won't either.) Just pick it up the next day, or put in some extra time when you can.

What matters is that you persevere and not give up. If you can hold to this pattern for just a few months, you'll have established a rewarding habit you can keep for life.

Memorizing Whole Books of the Bible

After using the Bible Memory File for some time, I'd memorized the majority of verses in a particular book of the Bible. So I decided to go ahead and commit the whole book to memory. It's not intimidating at all when you realize you can simply link up all the verses you already know by learning a few more in between.

To my delight, it was an overwhelmingly joyful process. I began to sense the scope and power of the Scriptures in a way I never had. I kept going, and whole books came alive. I gained insight into why the author would write what he did in a certain place and perhaps why he didn't include something in another place. My spiritual life was deepened and broadened beyond my greatest expectation.

One of the wonderful benefits of this stage of Scripture memorization was that the Spirit himself seemed to lead me daily in a process of development. He helped me learn as we went along. Now, on a six-week cycle, I can review all the books I've memorized and still tackle more. The beauty of it is that all I need to do is carry around a little pocket Bible (my "penknife," as opposed to a full-size "sword"). No more memory packs or files. Just the Scriptures.

The program I follow is to review the book on the day and week listed on a chart. When I first started, the chart looked like this:

	Monday	*Tuesday*	*Wednesday*	*Thursday*	*Friday*
Ephesians	1	2	3	4	5

As I learned more books of the Bible, it expanded to something like this:

Monday	Tuesday	Wednesday	Thursday	Friday
Ephesians	Galatians	Colossians	Philippians	2 Timothy

This led to the expanded, six-week cycle in which I go over all the books I've memorized while working on new ones. As I drive to church (which is about twenty minutes away), I can usually review three to five chapters of a book of the Bible. Once you get into it, it's not too hard.

I do sometimes slow down as I review these chunks of Scripture, taking time to meditate on them. And often I get a flash of insight or understanding.

Ultimately, though, Bible memorization is a matter of the heart. No one can stick with it whose heart isn't committed. It's something we do out of love for God, not because of pressure from pastor, group, or tradition. The methods I've provided here are meant only as a guide, a launching point, and hopefully an encouragement to internalize God's Word. Use it and develop it as the Spirit leads you.

The Ten-Second Prayer Principles

What does all this have to do with ten-second praying? The better you know the Bible, the more specific, wide-ranging, and fervent your prayers will become. And that will make you all the more effective in praying.

Recently, at the small-group prayer meeting I attend at my church, the leader asked each of us to share favorite passages from the Bible. Then she led us in praying those verses for each other and for the group.

One person mentioned Philippians 4:6–7, a passage familiar to many: "Be anxious for nothing, but in everything by prayer and supplication with thanksgiving let your requests be made known to God. And the peace of God, which surpasses all comprehension, will guard your hearts and your minds in Christ Jesus." Another person reminded us of Philippians 1:6, which says, "I am confident of this very thing, that He who began a good work in you will perfect it until the day of Christ Jesus." Psalm 119:11 was another mentioned: "Your word I have treasured in my heart, that I may not sin against You."

We began praying these Scriptures on behalf of each

other, and what a powerful time of prayer it turned out to be. It seemed our supplications were more fervent, more succinct and tightly drawn, and more joyous than they had been in some time.

That's the power of God's Word. Use it in your prayers, and you will be a ten-second prayer warrior indeed.

CHAPTER THIRTEEN

USING A PRAYER CYCLE

For most of us, the problem with prayer is that we don't seem to have enough to pray about. After we've asked God to bless our finances, give us favor with the boss when we give that crucial report on Friday, work out that little problem with our mother, and help us fill that assistant's position at work with a good, solid applicant, we draw a blank about what else we should be praying. Here we promised the pastor we'd pray for fifteen minutes a day every day—and we've only used up a minute and a half. What are we going to do with those other thirteen and half minutes—hum a catchy tune?

A prayer cycle can help us overcome these idea shortages.

What is a prayer cycle? I keep a folded, letter-size sheet of paper in my wallet. The cycle is basically just a list of people and things I pray for, but it fills both sides of that paper. I don't have a consistent, day-by-day method for doing this—I just pick up where I left off after the last time I used the list.

For instance, on the first round of my cycle, I've listed my family. So when I first start my prayer cycle, I pray for my family. Parents, sister, brother, uncles, aunts, grandparents, cousins: all of them. I don't always know what they need or what situation they're facing, but at least I mention them to God. "Please watch out for Paul, Lord. He's a rascal and tends to get into trouble. And help Aunt Shirley's knee operation to go well."

Next, if I still have time, I pray for missionaries I know from church and various other places. If I've seen their newsletters recently and know some of their needs, I'll pray specifically. At the same time, I praise God for their work and ask him to bless it. My list includes about ten missionaries, so I stop on each name, mention anything I know of that person's needs, and go on to the next.

After missionaries, I move on to neighbors: the Hortons across the street, the Starks next door, and all around my block. Since we live in a large community, I have plenty of people to pray for. I pray that some of them will meet and learn to love God. In the case of others, I pray for their kids. And for one neighbor, I pray about his dog: He's always getting out, and I'm worried he'll run into the street and get flattened. ("Please, Lord, don't let Molson get hit by a car!") I also pray that God will help me to share my faith whenever I have the chance.

If I'm still in the groove or have more time, I ask God to bless my church and meet the needs there: its ministry, pastor, other leaders, and specific members. "Help Vernon to preach up a storm, Father. Give him time to study and be accurate, and help him to throw in a joke now and then just to give us a laugh." It can be anything, really—whatever is on your heart.

After that, I pray for several churches in our community, along with those I used to attend in different areas of the country. I ask the Lord to lead the pastors of those churches. I may pray that he'll increase the attendance and keep them safe from crime and conflict.

The great thing about prayer cycles is that you can

stop whenever you need to, then pick up with the next item anytime you need a few good ideas to pray about. You can move through many important or even obscure subjects in your prayer times when you pray with the cycle. It can be a virtually endless source list of people, needs, and organizations, and situations to pray about. Here are some other items I pray about on various days:

- Christian organizations: Youth for Christ, International Bible Society, Campus Crusade for Christ, Billy Graham Evangelistic Association, InterVarsity, and others.

- That I may produce spiritual fruit: love, joy, peace, patience, etc.

- Christian magazines: *Discipleship Journal, Christianity Today, Marriage Partnership, Today's Christian Woman, World Magazine,* and their editors and publishers.

- That I may manifest spiritual qualities such as holiness, godliness, and truthfulness.

- Christian leaders: men and women from denominational seminaries; church elders and deacons; well-known leaders, like Dr. Howard G. Hendricks, Dr. Gene Getz, Dr. Charles Stanley, Dr. Charles Swindoll, and many others.

- Nations of the world: the United States, Canada, Mexico, Germany, and others.

- Friends at work.

- Friends from church.

- Sports personalities, such as Barry Bonds, Roger Clemens, Tiger Woods, Cal Ripken Jr., and Michael Jordan (I don't mind praying for retired athletes).

- Mainstream authors: Dean Koontz, John Grisham, Danielle Steel, and others.

- Christian authors: James Scott Bell, Jerry Jenkins, Bruce Wilkinson, and others.

- Christian publishing houses: Zondervan, Nelson, Multnomah, Howard Books, and others.

- Mainstream publishing houses: Random House, Simon & Schuster, Viking, and others.

- Television networks: CBS, ABC, NBC, FOX, CNN, and others.

- News anchors, local and national: Katie Couric, Charles Gibson, Brian Williams, and others.

- Actors and actresses: everyone I can name— Brad Pitt, Tom Cruise, Lindsay Lohan . . .

- Magazines: *Time, Newsweek, Cosmopolitan* . . .

- People in government: our president, vice president, senators, congresspeople, cabinet members, judges, and others.

- States and their governments: Missouri, Kansas, New York . . .

- Sports teams: the Royals and the Chiefs (my hometown teams), Bulls, Rams, and others.

See how this expands? You can divide the categories for different days and have someone or something different to pray about each day of the week.

After praying for actors and actresses in Hollywood, I was excited to hear that several had become Christians—Jane Fonda, Gary Busey, and Kirk Cameron among them. Did that happen just because I prayed? Probably not. But I believe I had some small part in their salvation because I prayed for them. That's gratifying.

Someone once told me about the Hollywood Prayer Network. A group of Christians in Hollywood have united to intercede for the film industry and the people involved in it. Hundreds of Christians are involved in moviemaking and would love to see God move in Hollywood.

Shouldn't Christians pray for the many people in all parts of our world? I believe so. And I think the more people we pray for, the more we'll see God work in their lives. Who knows? You may be the only person praying for a certain person, and one day in heaven you could learn that it was your prayers that moved God to draw that person to himself.

The joy of praying expansively for lots of people

through a prayer cycle is not just in seeing answers but in knowing that God, because he is all-knowing, sees the people we pray for—right now, where they are. He can work in their lives on the basis of the ten-second prayers we're sending up to heaven.

Several years ago I received a call from the editor of a book ministry. The moment he introduced himself on the phone, I knew who he was: I'd been praying for him for years as a part of my prayer cycle. I'd first met him in seminary and, at one point, rented a house with him and four other students. When I made up the list for my prayer cycle, I remembered him as a good friend and included his name. But I hadn't seen him since graduating from seminary in 1977.

Then, more than twenty years later (it was 1998), there I was speaking with him on the phone. He told me what he needed, and I promised I'd send him something. Then I said I'd been praying for him through the years. "I didn't know what you were doing or what you needed," I told him, "but I asked God to bless and keep you."

He laughed. "I wish I could say I'd been doing the same thing for you, my friend. But thanks. And God has blessed me richly over the years, especially in the last few, with this new ministry. So don't stop praying for me, and I'll remember to pray for you."

More recently I made an effort to reconnect with some of my comrades from college. I hadn't seen most of them since graduation in 1972, and I knew virtually nothing about many of them. Whenever I received our alumni newspaper, I eagerly scanned the articles looking for references to my friends and classmates, but usually I was disappointed. Names and faces I didn't know filled the pages. Those of people I longed for news about were absent.

Our alumni directory came out a few years ago, though, and it included e-mail addresses. So I sent messages to some old friends, hoping some might write back and we'd reconnect. Several did, all of them guys who also were on my prayer cycle and whom I'd prayed for through the years. I had the opportunity to share the gospel with some of them. One has kept up a regular e-mail correspondence, and we're hoping to reconnect at one of our college reunions. He hasn't become a Christian, but I've spoken to him about spiritual things. He listens, responds, and asks questions.

Being a prayer warrior involves much more than just praying for yourself. It means praying about the whole world, specifically and on target. One of the things a prayer cycle will do *in* you is to make you more aware of the needs of the world *around* you and motivate you to reconnect with some of the people who have long ago drifted out of your life. And when someone or something you've been praying for makes the news, you'll perk right up, wondering to what extent your prayers influenced that development.

Use the prayer cycle, and you might be surprised to learn how far-reaching the impact of your prayers can be—and how some of that power may come back to bless and change you.

CHAPTER FOURTEEN

MAKING A PRAYER FILE

I learned an important lesson about prayer from a rotten judge.

The corrupt fellow was featured in one of Jesus's teaching stories recorded in Luke 18:1–8. Luke introduced the parable by succinctly summarizing its point: "He was telling them a parable to show that at all times they ought to pray and not to lose heart" (Luke 18:1). In the Parable of the Unjust Judge, Jesus painted a picture of an official who repeatedly ignored the urgent and heartfelt pleas of a poor widow who entreated him for justice and protection from her adversaries. He had the power to help her; she had no power, except to petition him—which she did, again and again. In time her continual asking moved even this uncaring, unrighteous judge to act on her behalf.

Did he have a sudden change of heart, seeing the error of his ways and resolving to do right and fight for justice ever after? No. "He said to himself, 'Even though I do not fear God nor respect man, yet because this widow bothers me, I will give her legal protection, otherwise by continually coming she will wear me out'" (Luke 18:4–5). Jesus summed it up: "Will not God bring about justice for His elect who cry to Him day and night, and will He delay long over them? I tell you that He will bring about justice for them quickly" (Luke 18:7–8).

The unjust judge helped me realize that while we may need to offer some prayers only once, on other occasions we should "pester" God repeatedly. But how could I do that with so many needs out there and so many friends and people clamoring for God's help and my prayers?

More organization would help, I realized. And one of the best organizational tools I've discovered for use in my prayer time is something called the Prayer File. Using a three-by-five card filing system, I record prayer requests I receive from all kinds of sources and use the system to pray about a multitude of needs that I'd never be able to keep up with if I only used my lists.

Where did I get this idea?

When I attended seminary in the seventies, I got involved with some discipleship groups started by a doctoral student named Garry Friesen. He's an author and a college professor today, but back then he was developing a method for praying that I found immensely helpful.

The Prayer File works much like the Bible Memory File discussed in chapter 12. At the heart of the process is the three-by-five card file. You write each prayer request at the top of a three-by-five card, along with the date and where the request came from: the name of the person, organization, or event. When you learn that a particular prayer has been answered, record the answer on the corresponding card. Then move the card to a second file, for answered prayers.

Now back to the primary file for prayer requests. Make several divisions (using tabbed divider cards) into which to organize your prayer cards. In one section, file cards with requests you want to pray about daily. Highly important, pressing, and urgent needs belong in this section: a friend with cancer, a relative's marital problems, your crisis with the neighbors—whatever God impresses on your heart that's important enough to pray about every day.

Make a second division for needs you choose to pray about weekly. Within this section, label a tabbed divider for each day of the week, Sunday through Saturday. Divide up the prayer cards you want to pray about weekly (these are often less important, not-so-urgent matters, but ones you still want to pray for regularly) and distribute an equal number to the section for each day of the week. Then each day you can pull up the designated cards for that day and pray for the needs mentioned—like the spiritual needs of various neighbors and family members, your goals for the future, or projects you might be working on. Good weekly prayer subjects might also include missionaries, Christian organizations, and any other groups you're committed to praying for regularly but can't get to every day.

For the last division make thirty sections, one for each day of the month. Divide cards with requests you choose to pray for monthly between the thirty sections. These would be needs less pressing than any of the others and might include more distant acquaintances or organizations whose specific needs you don't even know as well as other topics that, while important, might not affect you as personally or come up as often as others.

As you can imagine, such a prayer file can get quite large. But that's the point. Through it you can pray about many different matters over long periods of time and keep on top of numerous prayer requests you'd otherwise forget. But in keeping with the Ten-Second Prayer concept, the Prayer File keeps the requests in manageable chunks that won't overwhelm even the busiest prayer warrior.

Here's how you can put it into practice. Each day, whenever you choose to pray—starting your walk, stepping into your bedroom (or other place) to pray or have a time of quiet supplication—grab the appropriate files: daily (same one every day), day of the week (for instance, Thursday), and day of the month (say, the eighth). Then just go through the cards one by one, offering a ten-second prayer about each. When God answers the prayer and meets the need, write down what happened and "retire" the card to your file of answered prayers.

That brings us to one especially beneficial feature of the file. Since I record just one prayer request per card, I have enough space to also write down the answer to the prayer whenever I receive it or learn of it. This has led to my keeping a much larger file of all the answers God has given me over the years. Now, in times of doubt or discouragement, all I have to do is take out that file and flip through the many cards I've kept throughout the years. This never fails to encourage me, for no matter how bad my situation might seem at the moment, I'm reminded the God I'm praying to now is the same God who answered back then. I'm reassured that he'll answer again in the future.

When I look back at my file of answered prayers, here are some of the wonderful answers that inspire to keep praying:

My Grandfather's Stroke

In the spring of 1973, when I'd been a Christian for less than a year, my grandfather suffered a serious stroke that left him bedridden in a nursing home, unable to walk or even talk. My grandmother crumpled into despair, saying over and over, "It's the end."

I had begun to truly believe in the power of prayer, and I took it upon myself to fast and pray for my grandfather. "Lord, please help Grandpa get better, and please help Grandma find some hope in the midst of this tragedy." I continued fasting and praying until I sensed God telling me he'd heard and was taking action.

My grandfather went on to walk again, talk without impairment, and drive his car—one of his greatest joys in life—for many more years. He was seventy-seven when he had his stroke. With God's help, he lived well into his nineties.

Custody Struggles for My Daughters

In 1991 I went through a difficult custody battle over my daughters. I really wanted to restore the marriage, but that didn't look possible. So gaining custody of the girls seemed paramount. However, I was powerless to change anything. My lawyer repeatedly told me that I'd never get custody as long as the kids appeared okay and healthy.

My constant prayer was that somehow God would make a way for me to get my girls back.

Then one Friday night I got a call from the police. They informed me that I had been charged with child abuse. A policewoman and a social worker would be conducting an investigation starting the following Monday.

I hung up the phone, terrified and enraged. I shook my fist at heaven and cried, "God, if this stands, you and I are finished."

An hour later I repented of my anger, but the fear remained. Although I knew the charges were baseless, I also knew how difficult it would be to prove innocence in a "he said/she said" situation. I was worried that the government would take away my kids permanently. Throughout the process, I prayed that God would work—in the investigators, in the psychologist assigned to the case, in the judge, in everyone involved.

Over the next few months, the investigators and the psychologist came to the conclusion that my kids should be with me. I won custody, and those two children were able to grow up in my household.

What might have happened if I hadn't prayed? If others hadn't prayed for me?

I'm not saying I'm a perfect parent, but I do believe the girls were better off with me. Both have grown up to be well-adjusted, responsible young women. I'm thankful God acted on their behalf—and mine. I'm thankful he still answers prayer today. And I'm thankful that because I have a written record of my situations, my prayers, and God's answers, I'll never forget that God answers my prayers. His answers still thrill me, and they always will.

Of course, keeping a prayer file like this goes beyond the immediate scope of ten-second praying and moves into the arena of regular, daily, and consistent times with the Lord in prayer. But that's the larger purpose of this book: to help you grow into that kind of lifestyle gradually, working into longer periods of prayer and intercession as you increase your praying power.

Just remember that this is no legalistic, grit-your-teeth, I'd-better-pray-today-or-I'm-in-trouble proposition. I'm convinced you'll want to pray more and more as you find how easy is it to pray for yourself, your family, and your world. And as you begin to see God's working through your prayers, the excitement and joy will encourage you to pray even more.

Adopt some of these methods, and you'll see amazing answers from God—in abundance. Isn't that what we all desire—to see God work in the world? Through these methods, not only can you see God's answers, but you just might be part of those answers.

CHAPTER FIFTEEN

A Final Word about the Importance of Prayer

If you read only one chapter of this book, this is the one I would want you to read, for it goes beyond methods to the heart of prayer and why we pray. Some of the methods I've outlined in previous chapters may seem a little unusual. Some of them may not be easily stitched into the fabric of your life. And some may seem too difficult for you to do on a regular basis. A few simply will not interest you, and you'll cast them aside. But it's my hope that you'll try several of these processes and find the ones most helpful to you.

One thing I've learned through my years as a ten-second prayer warrior is that I'm not perfect. I have good days and bad days. Some days I hardly pray a word. Prayer takes concentration and work, no matter how diligent we try to be, and Satan will do anything to derail our efforts. He constantly fights to keep us from entering into the spiritual battle with the power of prayer.

That's why I began abiding by an overriding principle in my prayer life—one that covers all the bases, whether I offer ten-second prayers every hour or not. This principle is simple: Pray about everything before the need arises, after it has come to your attention, and even after God has met the need.

This could be shortened to say, Pray about everything.

I'm often amazed at how easy it is to go through life without considering God's ways and plan. Too often I set off in the car or on a trip without giving the least thought to how God might be directing. For instance, when you and your spouse consider having a baby, you might not think of praying until you run into trouble: six months of trying and no conception. Unfortunately, we don't often begin with prayer. We only start praying when things go wrong. Prayer gets relegated to our option of last resort.

I've always hated that mentality, but I know it's standard operating procedure for many people, myself included. When I first started praying, I always asked for help with the big things: changing jobs, choosing a mate, deciding whether to move to another state, finding the right church. I rarely considered that God might want to be involved in the day-to-day small things as well: finding my missing keys or helping me retrieve the dog when he slipped out the front door and ran up the street.

Eventually, though, I realized, why not? Why shouldn't I pray about those little things? Maybe if I involved God right away, they wouldn't get out of hand. So I just began praying about everything, the moment it occurred to me. For instance, if I was driving down the street and remembered several things my wife wanted me to get at the store, since I couldn't write them down, I would pray: "Lord, help me remember the whole list so I don't miss anything."

It was a simple little thing. Some people might ask, "Why even pray about it?" But my attitude was, why not?

I have a problem remembering such things. They go in my head and right back out. So why wouldn't I enlist God's aid with such a problem? Did Jesus not say, "All things for which you pray and ask, believe that you have received them, and they will be granted you" (Mark 11:24)? *All things.* Doesn't that mean everything?

It's a difficult attitude adjustment for many people. For some reason we cling to the belief that God only wants to be bothered about the really significant things. But we're his children, and if the small things are causing us difficulty—like finding a parking space close to the mall entrance when it's raining, or needing your flashlight when you can't remember where you left it—why wouldn't he want to know about those too?

Some years ago, when my daughter Alisha was only eight or nine years old, we were cleaning her room. Her closet doors got jarred off the track in the process, so I went about fixing it. I talked aloud as I worked: "Okay, I have to be careful. There's a spring up there at the top, and I don't want to lose it." I jostled the door, it popped out, and the spring went *boing!*

Grumbling, I leaned the door against the wall and

began looking for the errant spring. I couldn't find it any-where. How far could it have sprung? It had to be in the room.

Then, remembering other such experiences, I prayed, "Lord, would you please help me find this stupid spring?!"

A moment later Alisha said, "Is this what you're look-ing for, Daddy?" She held the spring out to me.

I was astounded. It seemed God rarely worked in my life like this. But maybe the reason was that I didn't usu-ally pray about things like this.

On another occasion my wife decided she'd like to have an antique jukebox. I didn't think much about it, but when our giving to the church was current, the bills had been paid, we'd socked away some savings and even put some money into an IRA, I discovered we had some money left over—about a thousand dollars. So we began looking for a jukebox. At the time I didn't know about eBay, so the only place I could think to look was the classified ads. I prayed about it and went out to buy a paper.

That evening, when I opened the paper, what did I

find but an ad for a vintage jukebox in great condition and on sale for $1,500. That was still a little out of our price range, but I gave the seller a call. He told me all about his jukebox, and I promptly told Jeanette. We went to see it and offered the owner $1,000. He cocked his head, thought about it, and said, "Okay."

We had our jukebox. And I suspect God orchestrated the whole thing.

One time a friend of mine was rummaging through his clothes rack one night and pulled out a nice blazer. He was about to put it on when he sensed God telling him instead to take it to church and give it to a certain person.

My friend was used to such communications, and he did as God suggested. At church he walked up to the designated person and offered him the jacket. The man was stunned and said, "I've been praying about something exactly like this!"

Is God concerned about a lost spring, a sought-after jukebox, and a new sports jacket? I guess he is.

My experiences have taught me I should pray about everything: big things, little things, and everything in be-

tween, no matter how trivial I—or someone else—might
believe it is.

Because of so many occasions when God answered
my prayers about the small things, I find myself praying
about nearly every situation I face. Nothing elaborate. No
agonizing over whether it's God's will for me to pray. Just,
"Lord, I need this. Will you help?"

Not always, but more often than I can count, he
grants my request. It still astonishes me.

So I learned early on that God answers prayers about
the small things. But what about the big things—really
tough problems that I couldn't possibly handle on my
own or that would never happen by themselves were not
a big God working to make them happen? Could God
answer my prayers for such needs just as effectively?

It didn't take long for me to learn the answer: yes! I
became a Christian in August 1972 and promptly began
"bombing" my family with the gospel. My brother was
only amused, my sister taken aback. But my parents were
deeply offended, not only that I would suggest they
weren't Christians already, but that I could even question
that they might not be.

Over the next three years our relationship deteriorated. A wall grew between us, and though I stopped slamming them with the Bible and their need to seek Jesus, their fear that I might insert such issues into any conversation was evident. When I came home from seminary on school breaks, it seemed everyone tiptoed around me, never asking the deeper questions about my new life, never really giving me a chance to talk. It bothered me greatly, and I prayed about it constantly.

I couldn't have anticipated what God would do, but during my third year in seminary, I plummeted into the clinical depression I wrote about earlier in this book. Suddenly it felt as if God had disappeared from my life. I became a despondent, lost, broken, and hurting person who wanted little more than to sleep and get through my classes.

When I went home that year for Christmas, I had nothing to look forward to, nothing to celebrate. No one seemed to understand my feelings, and I couldn't explain them adequately. My father, though, was particularly attentive to me, and we often talked late into the night about how I was feeling. He repeatedly encouraged me not to drop out of seminary, which I was seriously considering, and not to give up on my goals and ambitions. He told me, "Someday you'll be through this, and you'll be glad you didn't throw in the towel."

I knew he was right, yet I couldn't believe it would ever happen.

My mom also spent a lot of time with me, giving me pep talks and assuring me: "Those wretched feelings were a long time coming, and will be a long time going; but they will go."

I came to depend on them both as my steady and constant encouragers.

Then one night my dad and I were driving home from a family gathering. I felt deeply despondent and didn't know what to say or do anymore. I felt on the verge of doing something desperate. It was then that my dad said, "Some years ago, I went through a depression a lot like what you're going through now."

I turned to him, astonished. My father rarely shared hard life experiences like that—or anything deeply personal. I asked him what had happened.

"You were in high school and probably didn't notice,"

he said, "but at Langston [the company he worked for] our president had been killed in an airplane crash, and the new guy who took over became my bitter adversary. He didn't believe that a product should be sold by real salespeople. He seemed to think the things would just sell themselves. Well, I was the sales manager, so I was the enemy. In meeting after meeting, he chewed me up. I went into a deep depression."

I was all ears. "What did it feel like? What happened to you?"

"It was like I was in this pit I couldn't get out of. At times I felt okay, but then suddenly, like someone just flicked a switch in my brain, I would slide into it. A lot of times I thought I'd never come out of it."

Of course, the burning question in my mind finally came out: "How did you get out of it?"

"For one thing, I changed jobs." He laughed. "That helped. But it took a while to feel like myself again. I had to fight it every day—fight giving in, fight the urge to fire a bullet into my brain, fight the horrible thoughts going through my mind. But gradually it started to lift."

"How long did it take?"

He shook his head. "About a year, maybe two."

I'd been in my depression for only three months. But you wouldn't believe how that conversation helped me. Not only had I reconnected with my father on an emotional level, but I knew he understood what I was facing. That gave me hope that he would help me through this horrid time.

During those years when I struggled, Mom and Dad wrote me letters, called frequently, sent money, and in general stood between me and oblivion in ways I can't adequately enumerate. Sometime during that process, I realized that God had answered my prayer: He had healed the rift between me and my parents. (The one between me and my brother and sister would take longer.) I was amazed and grateful, yet I had to ask: Why did it take a major depression to bring this about?

I didn't know. I only knew that God had brought some good from my depression. And that made me believe he might work in other difficult situations, which he certainly has.

More recently, my family decided to move from West Des Moines, Iowa, to Chicago because Jeanette had taken a job with *Moody* magazine. We had a lovely house in Iowa, certainly the best we'd ever lived in. Because we hadn't been able to sell our previous house in Maryland, my mother had lent me the down payment—more than 20 percent of the total cost of the house, so we wouldn't have to pay mortgage insurance. While we looked at homes in the Chicago area, our house in Maryland remained unsold, despite our many prayers about it, and now we had to sell another house in Iowa at the same time. Our real estate agent in Maryland assured us she was "on the cusp of a deal."

We visited the Chicago area over several weekends, and as we looked at the houses available in our price range, my heart sank. We soon discovered that to get a house like our Iowa beauty, we'd probably have to spend $70,000 to a $100,000 more than we had budgeted. I began thinking the move to Chicago was a foolish idea.

I worried a lot about paying back my mom and selling our house in Maryland. Both issues weighed heavily on my mind. Even if we did sell both houses in a close time frame, we still had to repay my mother's loan. That would leave us with barely enough to cover a down payment on a decent Chicago house.

I fretted about this for a while, but then Mom called one night. After the usual pleasantries, she got down to business: "I know you're worried about this loan thing, honey. And I want you to know, I don't expect you to pay me back right now. A house in Chicago will probably cost much more than one in Iowa. I'd rather you have a decent house than have you pay me back right away."

I was floored. I breathed a sigh of thanks to Mom and to God and thought about the possibilities. We went back to Chicago with real hope. Nonetheless, even looking at more expensive houses seemed fruitless. They were all dogs! I couldn't believe it.

Finally, in abject terror that we'd end up living in a dump, I fell to my knees one night and prayed. "Lord, I'm really disappointed at what we've seen in Chicago, but I truly believe you want us to go there; so please help us to find the right house. You know we need four bedrooms—each of the kids has their own bedroom now, and I don't want to take that away from them. We also need an office for Jeanette's and my freelance writing. We need a big garage—maybe a large two- door or a three-door for all the junk we have that Jeanette won't get rid of. The house also has to be in our price range." (I gave God a range, although I'm pretty sure he already knew.)

I took a deep breath, feeling I might be asking too much already, without what I was going to add next. "I'd really appreciate a finished basement . . . and it has to be a house we can entertain in, since I'll probably be pastoring somewhere. A fenced-in yard for the dog and the baby would also be nice."

I knew I was pushing it. I hadn't asked for something this big or this specific in years. But I finished, "Oh, and one last thing . . . I know this is stretching it, but maybe you could just surprise us with something extra about this dream house . . . I don't know what. Just a little surprise."

I took a deep breath and then said, "If I'm asking too much, I understand. May your will be done." That prayer lasted a little longer than ten seconds, but not every prayer should be confined to that time frame.

The next weekend we returned to Chicago. Our real estate agent gave us a listing of houses, and we looked through them. Several seemed promising but were well out of our price range. I really liked one, though. It had a four-car garage—bigger than we needed—but the house itself didn't look too big for us. It had a neat brick front and looked attractive, even genteel. It was nicely land-scaped. Best of all, it was just a little above our price range.

We visited the houses and came to the one I liked most. I was amazed. It featured three bedrooms upstairs, plus another room that served as a sitting room. The cov-eted features just kept adding up: an office on the main floor, a finished basement with a fifth bedroom, a fenced-in yard . . . it was perfect.

I walked around, absolutely in heaven. And then I dis-covered the surprise: a glassed-in sun porch with a hot tub. Now, I'm not really a hot tub kind of guy, but Jea-nette *oohed* and *aahed* over it, and the kids went bananas. Nicole took me aside, told me which bedroom she wanted and said, "Dad, you have to get this for me." Alisha also had her bedroom picked out and said, "Dad, I want that hot tub."

I felt astonished and overwhelmed. But the question was· Would the sellers come down to our price?

We went back to the realty office to draw up an offer. My real estate agent said, "We'll offer them twelve thousand less than they're asking. We'll probably get them to come down no more than two or three, but we'll have to wait and see."

I prayed again, we made the offer, and then we waited. The sellers answered the next day, agreeing to go down six thousand dollars! We countered with a raise of four thousand, they came down one more, and we said, "Yesss!" It was smack in the middle of the price range I'd prayed for.

That house was the greatest I'd ever lived in. And the same sort of thing happened again when we moved from Chicago to Kansas City a year and half later.

Frankly, I'm amazed at what God can and will do if we'll just ask. I'm not saying he'll do anything or everything. I'm not saying if you lose something he'll point you to it immediately. That's only happened a few times in my life. But I am finding that instead of waiting to pray as the "last resort" or "when everything else fails," we should immediately say, "Lord, will you please help me?"

As we learned in chapter 10, "The A-S-K Principle,"

many times God answers our prayers by having us do something to help bring about that answer. In the above situations I still had to look for the spring, search for a jukebox, and knock on some doors to get a house. Remember, Jesus said, "Ask, and it will be given to you; seek, and you will find; knock, and it will be opened to you" (Matthew 7:7). That says to me that sometimes God answers by getting us involved in being part of the answer—seeking and knocking, not just asking.

I'm also not saying that if you ask for some things—such as healing for an illness, the solution to a relational problem, or relief from some of the heavier burdens we bear in life—God will suddenly change everything for the better. God chooses which prayers he will answer, and how he answers them, and he always reserves the right to say no. But I've found that he often answers in several ways that offer hope. "Maybe," "Wait," "Perhaps later," or even "Let's think about it."

The point is that if we don't pray, how can we expect God to respond? Jesus told his disciples many times to pray, adding that they should never give up, because God is good and wants to meet all their needs.

Recently, in our small prayer group at church, we prayed about numerous situations, people, and needs. A tornado warning forced us to leave our comfortable quarters on the main floor of the church and seek shelter in the basement. We spent time praying about the threatening weather, but then we moved on to other pressing concerns:

- a father whose wife had died of cancer a year before, leaving him to raise three young children alone;

- another single father who wanted to adopt three children from foster care;

- a missionary in China suffering persecution;

- a woman diagnosed with cancer for the second time;

- a young man whose girlfriend had been killed in an auto accident a week earlier;

- a husband and wife whose newborn died only a few hours after birth;

- a child who was afraid of the dark and wouldn't sleep at night; and

- a high-school girl who ran away from home and was living with her boyfriend.

As I prayed that night, my heart was grieved. This was mind-boggling, heartrending stuff. What could be done to help these people? Humanly speaking, not much could be done to change their situations or bring them comfort. But we were praying to a God powerful enough, loving enough, and interested enough to help every one of those people. I was confident he not only knew their needs but also knew the best way to meet them. With joyful confidence, I cried out to a Lord whom I trusted would do right by all those folks.

What would I do if I didn't have God like that? What if the God I believed in had no power to help, no control over the situations, or no desire to change things? What if my God couldn't speak to, comfort, help, guide, teach, or do any number of other miracles Christians experience daily?

I know what I would do if my God were this weak. I'd give up on him. I'd find another god. I'd go somewhere else. I'd search in Buddhism or Islam or something else for someone I could entrust with the grave problems of my life and those of others.

But the truth is that our God is sovereign, he's present, and he's prepared to act on our behalf. He's out there—watching, listening—with plans for each one of us, to bless us, to keep us, to make his face shine upon us, and to be gracious to us. He can work in and change human conditions and situations. He can speak to a man whose name I don't even know who has suddenly found himself a single father of three little kids. That man is miles away from me even as I pray in my little room in Liberty, Missouri. But God knows him—and cares.

God can comfort a young man whose first love was stripped from him in a horrible accident.

God can work in the life and situation of that missionary in China who I'll likely never meet until our paths cross in heaven.

Our God is a God who can change lives, situations, hearts, and events. Our God is a God with limitless power. He can and will act on the basis of every prayer you and I ever pray.

That's the God who *is*. And that's the God Joseph believed in even when everything had gone wrong in his life. He's the God Moses pleaded with for help when he led the vast and difficult group of Israelites out of Egypt and through the wilderness. He's the God Paul spoke with daily and who used Paul to turn the world upside down. He's the God who through the centuries has led Christians to glory, even if in this world it meant death in the arena or burning at the stake. He's the God who will lead your life—if you give him that privilege. And he's the God who will take you on as a special and beloved friend, who will bless you in this life and then take you to heaven to be with him forever. He will enable you to pray for your friends, your brothers and sisters, and your enemies, even in the face of death and loss. He'll lead you to pray about things you honestly think are impossible.

But God has the power to do the impossible . . . and he has the concern for you to do it.

Why? Because he is a God who loves each of us more than we can ever imagine or hope. Because he is a God who longs to hear from you and to answer the prayers you offer tonight, tomorrow, and every day for the rest of your life.

You can be a true ten-second prayer warrior.

Don't give up.

Keep trusting.

Keep asking.

Keep seeking.

Keep knocking.

And don't listen to what the world and the devil are telling you. God will answer. One day you'll know the countless things he did as a result of *your* prayers.

So get praying. Ask the Spirit to prompt and remind you. Use the tools in this book to get you going and keep you on track. And know that I'm with you, somewhere in this world, kneeling before the same throne of grace and anticipating that God will do amazing things in our lives and our world because you and I have asked him.

A Little Reminder about Praying with Others

When I pray in small groups, or even large ones, I try to abide by a few guidelines you also may want to consider adopting:

- Pray briefly. Don't try to impress anyone with your eloquence. Get in and get out.

- Pray specifically. Avoid broad generalities like, "God bless Africa." Try to name some specific need or request for God to answer.

- Do most of your worship on your own time. Some people spend a lot of the group prayer time praising the Lord with broad statements like, "God, you're awesome. You're great. You're magnificent"—all true but so general that they don't really say much. Try to be specific here, too, but always brief.

■ Don't judge the way others pray. Sometimes I have to fight to keep my mind in the attitude of prayer it should be in. It seems Satan is always whispering in my ear commentary on the prayers of others. "What an idiot!" "Come on, stop blathering on and end already." Or, "Just spit it out, will you?" Recognize the dark source of such thoughts and refuse to dwell on them.

■ Pray with others as they pray. I often silently "echo" others' prayers: "Yes, Lord, I second that one. Please answer this one speedily." Or, "Lord, I concur. I think this is a real problem that needs some powerful answers."

Over the years I've been a part of many small and large group prayer times. Some were boring. Some were attended by saints whose prayers went on and on and on. In others I had to struggle to keep a right attitude. Then again, perhaps some people don't enjoy my style of praying. We all have our own preferences and hang-ups, and it can be easy to let those distract us in a group prayer setting. So one of the most beneficial ways I've found to pray in a group is simply to talk to God in your mind when you're not voicing a prayer aloud and concentrate on being a conduit for the thoughts of the Spirit. Let God speak to your heart, and respond. Carry on a conversation.

Praying in groups can be fulfilling and fun. And don't forget to get all your prayer-group members to read this book—that would be an answer to *my* prayers.